Answers to Relational Healing 101

Answers to Relational Healing 101

Including Testimony and Teaching of Freedom from Homosexuality

Pamela R. Poston

Copyright © 2015 by Pamela R. Poston. All rights reserved.

No part of this book may be reproduced in any written, electronic, recording, or photocopying without written permission of the publisher or author.

Scripture quotations marked (AMP) are taken from the Amplified® Bible, Copyright © 1954, 1958, 1962, 1964, 1965, 1987 by The Lockman Foundation. Used by permission. (www.Lockman.org)

Scripture quotations marked (ASV) are taken from the Holy Bible, American Standard Version. Text courtesy of BibleGateway.com

Scripture quotations marked (KJV) are taken from the Holy Bible, King James Version. Text courtesy of BibleGateway.com

Scriptures quoted from THE HOLY BIBLE, NEW INTERNATIONAL VERSION®, NIV® Copyright © 1973, 1978, 1984, 2011 by Biblica, Inc.® Used by permission. All rights reserved worldwide.

Scripture quotations marked (NLT) are taken from the Holy Bible, New Living Translation, copyright ©1996, 2004, 2007, 2013 by Tyndale House Foundation. Used by permission of Tyndale House Publishers, Inc., Carol Stream, Illinois 60188. All rights reserved.

Scripture quotations marked (TLB) are taken from The Living Bible copyright © 1971. Used by permission of Tyndale House Publishers, Inc., Carol Stream, Illinois 60188. All rights reserved.

Front Cover Image Designed by: Andrey Navrotskiy/123RF.COM
Back Cover Image Designed by: Anastasiia Sochyvets/123RF.COM
Cover Designed by the author.
Advisor and Managing Editor: Overseer Walter L. Poston
Publisher: Dream Big Publishing, a division of Dream Big Enterprises, LLC and Highways and Hedges Outreach Ministries (www.Highways4JC.com)

ISBN-13: 978-0692394298 (Dream Big Publishing)
ISBN-10: 069239429X
1. Relational Healing–Biblical Teaching 2. Homosexuality –Religious aspects–Christianity. 3. Self-help. I. Poston, Pamela R. II. Title

Although every precaution has been taken to verify the accuracy of the information contained herein, the author and publisher assume no responsibility for any errors or omissions. No liability is assumed for damages that may result from the use of information contained within.

Printed in the United States of America

DISCLAIMER

This is a work of creative nonfiction information. The events are portrayed to the best of Pamela R. Poston's memory. While all the information in this book is true, some names and identifying details have been changed to protect the privacy of the people involved. This book is designed to provide information on basic relational healing and wholeness. This information is provided and sold with the knowledge that the publisher and author do not offer any legal, physiological, medical, or other professional advice. In the case of a need for any such expertise, consult with the appropriate professional. This book does not contain all information available on the subject of relational healing and wholeness. This book has not been created to be specific to any individual's or organizations' situation or needs. Every effort has been made to make this book as accurate as possible. However, there may be typographical and or content errors. Therefore, this book should serve only as a general guide and not as the ultimate source of subject information. This book contains information that might be dated and is intended only to educate and for points of interest. The author and publisher shall have no liability or responsibility to any person or entity regarding any loss or damage incurred, or alleged to have incurred, directly or indirectly, by the information contained in this book. You hereby agree to be bound by this disclaimer or you may return this book in its original form within the guarantee time period for a full refund.

DEDICATIONS

I dedicate this book to my loving husband, Overseer and Sr. Pastor Walter L. Poston! The Lord has blessed me with one of His very best, who brings out the best in me. Honey, I love you very much and we make an awesome team. Thank you for your selfless Love in serving our country as a U.S. Army Veteran and being a true Man of God. I am humbly grateful how you have made many provisions for me to take this faith walk and complete this book. You are indeed my HERO!

In loving memory of my Mom and Dad, I dedicate this book to you both, for giving me natural life. Dad, I salute you for serving and protecting our USA as a Navy Veteran. Thank you both for praying, fasting, and believing God for my new-birth in Christ Jesus; because it is He who gave me spiritual life, healing, and wholeness. Mom and Dad, I truly appreciate your uncompromised LOVE!

I dedicate this book to all of my readers, supporters and especially to individuals behind the wall. May your Relational Healing and Wholeness be contagious!

Jimmie F. Taylor, may you rest in peace.

Epigraph

This book is a tribute to:

God the Father
God the Son
God the Holy Spirit

for setting me FREE!

So if the Son liberates you [makes you free men], then you are really and unquestionably free.

John 8:36 (AMP)

Acknowledgements

When I set to write this acknowledgement and concluded with four pages of names and accolades, I know I was in trouble. This journey took a decade, with countless individuals contributing in so many ways. How do you honor innumerable amounts of individuals who prayed, mentored, edited, inspired, encouraged, influenced, supported, submitted their questions and for those who cheered me on to complete this book, without failing to mention someone's name?

Therefore, to all of my family, friends and acquaintances; your love and support is deeply appreciated in making this prophetic word and dream come true.

Thank You!

Contents

Introduction / 10

1. *My Testimony:*
   Rescued by Repentance from a Love Triangle / 14

2. *Facing the Facts - Applying TRUTH for*
   Relational Healing with God and Others / 46

3. *Relational Matters -*
   I'm at a Crossroad, Which Way Do I Go? / 64

4. *Homosexuality -*
   "HELP" I'm having An Identity Crises / 94

5. *STD's in Our Communities -*
   Sexually Transmitted Demonic Spirits / 130

6. *Intimacy -*
   When the Enemy is "My Inner Me" / 149

7. *Relational Lies -*
   Deception, Deceivers & being Deceived / 161

8. *Childhood Abuse -*
   I Was Only a Child - Y' Me? / 176

9. *The Signs of the Time -*
   My Way or God's Way / 183

10. *Healed, Now What? -*
    You can be "Unquestionably Free!" / 192

11. *Questions to the Author / 218*

12. *Explanatory Notes / 227*

Introduction:

Have you ever had questions concerning having a relationship with God, with people, or within yourself? Did you desire a short, but precise answer? Here in the United States of America, everyone has an opinion, since we are a liberal nation. However, have you ever wonder what God has said about a matter? Wouldn't it be wonderful to find these answers without the need to read the entire bible?

These 78 power pack answers will be a great start to many of those hard to ask questions concerning relational matters.

When an individual is wronged in anyway, the level of hurt and pain may go so deep that only a Holy God can heal. We see behaviors of individuals, but in reality what we see isn't their problem at all. So often, these are fruit (actions / behaviors) of their pain. The roots sometimes go so deep in their soul, even their mind do not want to comprehend its trauma. Only when the life-line of that root is severed and the fruit is plucked, then true relational healing and wholeness can take place.

Introduction

A profound writer, the Apostle Paul stated; *"When I was a child, I spake as a child, I understood as a child, I thought as a child: but when I became a man, I put away childish things"* (1 Corinthians 13:11 KJV). This author shared that the way we communicate, understand, and think will be different as an adult, versa as a child. Each of us should be developing and maturing in these three areas as we go through the process of the developmental stages of life. By the time an individual reaches adulthood, their personality and character should be shape; their ability to speak, understand, as well as their thought patterns should be developed.

Medical professionals have concluded, our various life experiences help to shape us into the person we become. It is suggested that our family and social interactions play a major role in the development of our personalities.

Think about how your mother and/or father taught or demonstrated ways to have relationships with them and your siblings; these life lessons molded your morals, values, and the way you view family structure. Consider the different communities where your family lived. Remember how your elementary school teacher attempted to inspired you to become a teacher, banker, fireman, lawyer, etc. Even some of your friendships inspired or uninspired your life decisions. These experiences were part of your development. They affected the way you thought; including the decisions and choices you made for your life. It is through these kinds of relational experiences that you form an opinion about yourself.

God so beautifully created the rainbow; to establish a covenant with every living creature. *He promised not to destroy the earth again with a flood* (Genesis 9:15). The hues are so wonderfully layered in harmony. He even set a rainbow around His throne (Revelation 4:3). His desire for humanity is similar to a rainbow; demonstrating how we can walk in harmony with Him and one another. Therefore, each time you see a rainbow in the sky, on a flag or within a picture; remember God's covenant with us (Genesis 9:17).

My desire is that you discover how much you are loved and valued. Then come into an understanding that your life is precious and worth more than all the riches of the world. I love you, but God sent Jesus to prove that He loves you best.

My Testimony:
Rescued by Repentance from a Love Triangle

Who wants to be a millionaire? I did, I met and later married an Illinois Lottery millionaire.

Jimmie was a loquacious older gentleman I met while shopping one afternoon for items I needed for an upcoming trip to Phoenix, AZ. We met after I parked my red hot firebird in a parallel parking space in a Chicago South Side shopping area one sunny afternoon. As I exited my car, a single red rose placed in my front window caught his attention and he said, *"Wow, that rose reminds me of my mother!"* He spoke of his mother's coffin he remembered as a little boy, at her funeral. His grandfather would not allow any other flowers on his daughter's coffin but a single red rose.

We were immediately intrigued with one another after meeting and remained friends until the next year. Then we began a romantic relationship until we eloped in Las Vegas, NV three years later. It was a cold sunny afternoon in March. We went to the *We've Only Just Begun Wedding Chapel*; a quaint little white chapel built in 1976, north of the famous Las Vegas Strip. Shortly thereafter, we had a lavish wedding on the busy South Shore Boulevard Street in our hometown Chicago, IL; so our family and friends could celebrate with us.

Our marriage was a beautiful arrangement as we fulfilled one another's dreams and ambitions. One of my dreams was to live in a warm climate; to escape the frigid winters in Chicago. So we returned to sunny Las Vegas a year later and decided to relocate there. We had a beautiful home with custom made furniture located in *"The Lakes"* a quiet prestigious western community, built around a large private man-made lake named, *"Lake Sahara."*

The first few years of marriage were wonderful, until I became bored and starting to feel God nudging and tugging on my heart and soul. I realized I had an empty void I could not seem to fulfill deep down within me. I felt this emptiness a few years prior, but I thought being married to a millionaire was the missing piece of my life's puzzle. Jimmie bought me a luxury convertible car when I finished fashion design school. He bought me fine jewelry, and furs; I traveled abroad and still could not fulfill this empty void. I tried several hobbies, career changes, met new friends of which some were rich and famous, including other life adventures; but nothing could seem to fulfill this empty void in my soul.

I later thought, *"Maybe if I would spice up my life with a female partner on the side, this would fulfill me."* Remembering as a youth growing up in church, I had a fondling session at a church girl's home as her parents slept in another room. Then in college, I had my first sexual female experience with a schoolmate from Illinois I met on a fashion field trip in Paris, France. We secretly had several romantic affairs prior to my marriage to Jimmie.

As my longing for female companionship grow, I sought to find a female partner; since all of my family and friends were back in Chicago. After several dates with women through dating services, newspaper ads, and strip clubs; I thought I got lucky. I met a female who was a Las Vegas native; which is rare in Las Vegas, from a *"Female seeking Female"* newspaper ad. I will call her, *"Girl A"* to protect her identity. Our attractions for one another immediately exploded. After committing adultery with her, we agreed to start a romantic relationship and move from Las Vegas to

Southern California. So, I planned a premeditated argument with my husband, packed my things then I moved out, and we were on our way.

As we entered into the small Southern California town of Hemet, I remember passing a little community church thinking, (*maybe we could worship there together as a couple in this charming little town*). Shortly after settling in, life happened and we never made it to that little community temple of worship.

She started a new job as a manger of a local fast food restaurant, which paid her well. She gave me her paychecks to pay bills and handle household needs. We lived comfortably for a while until my conscience started to get the best of me about living my adulteress and sinful lifestyle.

After a while, I felt God nudging and tugging on my heart and soul once again. I knew my choice to live in a homosexual lifestyle and adultery was selfish. This decision had me so rebellious and against God's instructions, but I wanted to do things my way. My conscience kept reminding me that I was: *breaking the first ordained order that He gave to mankind for sexual affiliations and marital unions,* but I didn't care. Girl A and I talked about our lifestyle on several occasions trying to ignore its eternal consequences. We both had parents that taught Christian values at home; my dad an ordained Deacon and my mom an ordained Evangelist. As fate would have it, Girl A was a Preacher's daughter. I remember meeting a Christian in a gas station who witnessed the gospel of Jesus Christ to me and gave me a lovely book, free of charge; but by then, my heart was too hardened to read it.

As time passed, we went through many relational struggles and battles trying to make our relationship work. Arguments started with several breakups, infidelity, financial struggles, crime and being on the run for seventeen months, then our suicide attempts.

Okay, if you are like me and like details you're probably asking yourself, *"Did I miss something here; did she just say 'crime and being on the run for seventeen months?' Wait, give me details please."*

After one of my breakups with Girl A, I decided to leave her in California and move back to Las Vegas hoping to reconcile my marriage. Feeling guilty and condemned, I crumbled under the pressure of my conscience for leaving my husband for this adulterous relationship.

When I called to inform Jimmie I was coming back home, he sounded excited. However, he did not display his anger of me leaving him until I arrived back to our Las Vegas home. After a few days, it was one argument after another. One night an argument was so heated that I refused to sleep in our master bedroom with him, so he dragged me from one room to another. Then things escalated, he threatened to kill Girl A and me. He described it so horribly and said, "*He would murder us or pay to have us killed, bury our bodies in the Las Vegas desert so deep that no one would find us for decades!*"

After this argument, he turned off the bedroom lights, left our room to watch sports in another room. While he was away watching television, I could hear sounds coming from the kitchen that he was still furious and brewing. Fear gripped me as I remembered; he had two guns in the house. I searched anxiously in the dark bedroom for those guns. I found one in his nightstand and held on tight; remembering one past New Year's Eve, he taught me how to shoot it. Then I slowly pulled back the safety clip and slid my finger onto the trigger as I nervously held the gun close to me while lying in the bed and waiting for his return. I thought I was pretty knowledgeable how to use it from a past New Year's Eve shooting lesson, but apparently not.

After a while which seemed like hours, I heard him coming into our bedroom. When I saw his shadow, I thought; *I would shoot straight up into the ceiling warning him that I meant business as well.* Sin had me so blind by then. The devil told me to shoot in the air like the cowboys, which always got everyone's attention. As his shadow came closer the devil spoke to me even louder, *"No shoot him, shoot him because he's coming to get you!"* Then the devil told me, *"Don't you let him kill you because then he's going after your woman, shoot him!"*

Aiming toward the ceiling I fired, "**POW**" as the loud sound rang my eardrums they began to go numb. A flash of lightning struck the gun's barrel as one bullet (*faster than the speed of sound*) quickly left the chamber into the air to its unknown destiny. Things went silent, no movement, no talking, just silence as gunpowder filled the air. I wondered, *"Where did he go, did he get me first, did I die, oh no- am I dead!?"* Things happened so fast!

When I came to myself, I was still lying in the bed; with the gun in my hand, in our dark bedroom. I jumped up and turned on the bedroom light to find the bullet did not go into the ceiling as I intended. It went into my husband's neck! *"Yes, in his neck!"* I screamed and thought, **"Oh my God, I know better than this, I've gone too far!"**

I was terrified, panicking and pacing the bedroom floor as I watched him sliding down the bedroom wall. He was holding his neck as blood was dripping on the carpet. Then with his very faint voice he mumbled, *"Why did you shoot me, I wasn't going to hurt you, I'm sorry."* I cried as I quickly and anxious prayed, *"God please do not let him die, please do not let him die!"*

I ran to the phone and called 911. The paramedics and police arrived within minutes. The paramedics sedated him and took him away. The police questioned me for a while and left. *Yes, they left me at home.* I called my female partner, packed as much as I could get into my convertible BMW 325i and fled!

As I fled and now finding myself on the run for the next 17 months, I ended up back in Hemet, California. After arriving there, I called my parents and they were gravely disturb about this incident and advised me to come back home to Chicago. I refused my parents request, because I did not want to leave my relationship with Girl A. I did not want to leave her alone in Hemet, fearing Jimmie would locate and harm her.

After a while, I became employed at a well establish medical supply company. I returned my leased BMW and we bought a different car, so it would make it difficult for Jimmie or anyone else to find us. I remembered as we came home from work one day and saw a car in our apartment complex parking lot that looked like Jimmie's car, we fled! We eventually moved from that complex, into a townhome community in another part of Hemet. Fear was now getting the best of me; however I heard nothing from Jimmie or about him for a while.

I met a female coworker and we hit it off very well (I will call her "*Girl O*" to protect her identity). Overtime, we became friends and Girl A noticed our friendship was becoming a threat to our relationship. Arguments started over her, distrust, then break up threats. Finally, we just decided it was time to call it quits.

After this relationship ended, I realize it was the effectual prayers of our parents, which kept us from our destructions and demise. I now know that I went through all of this because of my rebelliousness, pride and stubbornness against God.

I moved back to Las Vegas to get my life back on track and to live by myself, free from everybody. I found wonderful employment at a prominent Las Vegas Hotel and Casino in the heart of the Las Vegas Strip. It was a well-paid position and because of my work performance, I received a promotion as Relief-Supervisor of the VIP room reservations department. I moved into a very cute one bedroom loft apartment, not far from work. Things were starting to shape up and my future was starting to look bright.

Jimmie found out that I was back in Las Vegas. Thankfully, he was making a full recovery from the gunshot wounds. We talked on the phone several times and he shared that he forgave me, so things were cordial. He asked if we could get together and talk about reconciling. I refused and he did not take that very well.

Weeks later, another call came from Jimmie, asking if we could get together. When I refused he asked, "*So you don't want to get back with me because of those lesbians?*" When I told him that he could not control me and I could do what I wanted to, he lost it!

Well by now, I kept refusing him because Girl O and I were getting better acquainted long distance. She was planning to come to town and I didn't want him involved in this mixture. I was then falling in love with her.

Now months later, when Jimmie and I spoke again he tried once more. After my refusal, he threated to come to my apartment and finish what I did not. He said something like: *this time it would not be him, who would encounter a bullet, but it would be me and if a female was there then she would be included too!*

I called a homosexual male friend in Los Angeles, CA and he came to Las Vegas. When he arrived, we went to a local pawn shop on the Las Vegas Strip and he helped me pick out a gun for protection. I did not call the police because I thought I could handle my own business, my way. I thought, *Well I got away with shooting him the first time, so the law would understand if I have to do it again to protect myself.*

Not knowing, my crime was about to catch up with me. So, I chose a gun and was told, *since I was a first-time handgun buyer I must wait 72 hours after my purchase before I can pick it up.* I was fine with that since my friend was in town and I felt safe being with him.

Before the crack of dawn and before I heard the birds chirp on that April early morning, **BAM-BAM-BAM,** sounded on my door as I startled and awoke. I hurried to the door, hoping it would not awake my guest upstairs. Then, to find out who was knocking on my door so early and so loud!

When I asked, "*Who is it?*" they replied, "*It is the Las Vegas Metro Police Department!*" I thought they were at the wrong apartment until they said, "*We are looking for Pamela Taylor, open this door!*" When I opened the door, my apartment complex was surrounded with plain clothed Metro Police! They stormed into my apartment and began searching it looking for weapons. They awaken my guest and searched him, then his name to ensure he wasn't wanted for any crimes as well. They found me at my apartment because of the gun registration at the pawn shop.

I was told I was being arrested for, "***Attempted Murder and Battery with a Deadly Weapon***" because of the crime 17 months earlier on Jimmie! They handcuffed me and transported me to the Clark County Detention Center – Las Vegas city jail. My one phone call was to Jimmie asking him, "*Why did you press charges against me?*" He explained that he did not, but the State of Nevada pressed charges for the crime committed in their State.

I pleaded with Jimmie to get me out of jail, so he felt sorry for me and hired me an attorney. He and the attorney met prior to my meeting with him at the jail. The attorney counseled me before my court appearance. I then pleaded with God; *to get me out of this mess and promised Him if He did, I would turn from my sinful ways.*

The next day was my scheduled court appearance. I was escorted to the courtroom by several officers; shackled hands, waist and feet together with a line of other men and women. As we set waiting for our cases to be called before the judge, I witnessed him sentencing the majority of the offenders' jail and prison time.

When my name was called, my limp body arose. I was so afraid and weak by then in fear of the penalty for my crimes. My attorney stood to represent me before the judge. As they conversed for a few moments, the squeaky courtroom door opened. My attorney turned and looked, then stated to the judge: *the victim in question, just arrived.* The judge asked Jimmie to approach the bench and he was sworn in.

Jimmie testified that: *I was the perpetrator of these crimes in question.* He then shared: *my life was transformed and I was a new person now.* He also told the judge*: I became a Christian and left the homosexual lifestyle, which caused our marriage problems.* I was in shock as I listened to his testimony of this new person that I didn't know. The judge was relieved to know that he was recovering from his injuries, but was concerned about his safety. The judge thanked him for his testimony and wished him well. He was dismissed.

After Jimmie's testimony, the judge shared with my attorney that he needed to give some further thought about my case. The judge expressed his concerns about the seriousness of the charges against me. He requested to have another appearance with my attorney and me later that day.

After all of the cases were completed, we were escorted back to our holding cells. While in the jail cell, I then pleaded with God once more, this time more intensely. *"Lord God, I know you can answer prayer because I have seen you do it so many other times for my parents and me, as well as others."* This time I promised God, *"If you get me out of this mess, I promised I would turn from my sinful ways and leave the homosexual lifestyle."* Later that day, my attorney and I reappeared before the judge. He ruled that I should be released on my own recognizance, with psychiatric evaluations, and a period of time to stay out of trouble. If I did not comply, I would be mandated to appear before the judge again, but at this appearance he would sentenced me to serve prison time.

It was some experience I went through in jail; being subjected to food fights, arguments, the chain gang experience, humiliation, and losing my freedom.

God rescued and showed me that He can be a lawyer in the courtroom! He showed me His loving mercy and grace, through a Las Vegas Justice Court

Judge - who did not sentence me to the prison time I was facing. Yes, I was guilty of this crime and being on the run for 17 months. I would have deserved the penal system's punishment, but God's Love toward me set me free! Nine and a half weeks later, after being released, completing psychiatric evaluations and staying out of trouble; I was cleared from both felony charges. Praise Jesus!

It wasn't until years later, when I shared my testimony with our tax person (who is a Christian Believer); she interpreted my jail experience to me. She said: *Jimmie's testimony wasn't a lie.* God allowed him to prophecy my life through his testimony to the judge. Because God honors His covenant in Holy Matrimony, He allowed Jimmies' testimony to cover me from prison time. She also shared: *God knew in the future, I would become that Christian woman, who would leave the homosexual lifestyle that he testified about.* **"Today, I am that woman!"**

Well, the devil wasn't finish with me yet. I called Girl O after my release from jail and she came to Las Vegas to visit me. We started a romantic long distance relationship. Doing things my way again overtime, her charisma started to pull on my flesh and she won. Months later, I packed up all of my belongings and left Las Vegas again. I moved to Fallbrook, a beautiful northern town in San Diego County, California to live with her.

I was convinced that I found true love this time. I thought: *I am finally living the wonderful lesbian lifestyle I so longed for.* She had a wonderful job and I found employment at another lucrative medical company close by her home. She wined and dined me, treated me like a story book lover which made me turn my back on God as well as all my promises to Him, Jimmie and my good job in Las Vegas. I truly believed *(this was the relationship of a lifetime).*

We made one commitment after another to each other. After a while, we took it further and went to Honolulu, Hawaii to have a double commitment ceremony on the ocean front with another gay male couple (*my male friend who came to Las Vegas and kept me safe from Jimmie's threats*). I legally changed my last name to hers. We wore Hawaiian custom made ceremony rings as wedding bands to secure our life commitment to one another. We had a beautiful reception with many friends from the homosexual community who gathered to celebrate with us at a Los Angeles dance hall when we returned from Hawaii.

We began investing even deeper into our relationship. She bought me another car, clothing, jewelry; we traveled and did a lot of fun things with our friends in the gay community. They were affluent, pleasant and friendly individuals. We went to fun lesbian group gatherings, parties at their homes and their horse ranch estates. Life finally seemed really good and I was in love!

Thinking about all of the Las Vegas jail drama I left, my failed marriage because Jimmie then divorced me and escaping all of my promises to God, made me feel like I escaped it all. I also thought: *this relationship will fill that empty void I've had so long in my soul; because I convinced myself that she felt like my soul-mate.* I know now, what it means when the Bible says: "*Sin is pleasurable for a season*" (Hebrews 11:24-26).

God was at work after all. After a while, night after night, I would have dreams about the world coming to an end with great destruction. I would dream about the horrid of Hell with much fear, fire, darkness torment, and damnation there. I explained to Girl O that my love for her just could not withstand the tugging God now had on my heart and soul. She did all she could do in her strength to prove to me that our relationship could make it, if I just gave her more time.

I assured her that I would make this relationship work and we would be happy. I promised I would fight for us to make it *(because the emptiness started coming back inside of me)*. I tried so hard to hold on to her and ignore God. I remember making a bold statement to her that: *"I was willing to go to Hell when I die just to stay with you!"* My heart was hardening against God, but He was long-suffering with me and He would not let me go!

Over those years, I tried so many times to break free from sin; but I could not in my own strength. My attempts took me from one woman to another woman *(like a dog retuning to its vomit, according to Proverbs 26:11)*. I went deeper and deeper into one level to another level of sin which almost killed me and had me attempt murder on my husband. At times, my sins made me feel like I was in a bucket with crabs. I felt I was being pulled back into deeper sins unto my demise!

Sin took me so low to abuse a wonderful marriage, several suicide attempts, lost blessings that the devil stole, escaped two Category B felonies which could have been a maximum range of 8 to 20 years in prison for each charge, but GOD! I now know that this was all from not obeying God and doing things my way. I kept finding myself back where I had started, being enslaved to my own sins. Then the devil brought me love in a lovely woman who God did not intend for me to have as a lover. Someone who made me feel complete for a season, but my soul was empty and lost. A person that I made a vow to go to Hell to have her, but God said: **"NO!"**

The Lord finally got my attention through my mother. She and my dad attended bible study one evening. Their Pastor asked her to turn to a random scripture anywhere in her Bible and she landed on Ezekiel 3:17-21.

Ezekiel 3:17-21 (TLB)

[17] "Son of dust, I have appointed you as a watchman for Israel; whenever I send my people a warning, pass it on to them at once.

¹⁸ If you refuse to warn the wicked when I want you to tell them, 'You are under the penalty of death; therefore repent and save your life,' they will die in their sins, but I will punish you. I will demand your blood for theirs.

¹⁹ But if you warn them, and they keep on sinning and refuse to repent, they will die in their sins, but you are blameless—you have done all you could.

²⁰ And if a good man becomes bad, and you refuse to warn him of the consequences, and the Lord destroys him, his previous good deeds won't help him—he shall die in his sin. But I will hold you responsible for his death and punish you.

²¹ But if you warn him and he repents, he shall live, and you have saved your own life too."

Their Pastor interpreted it and told her to: *warn all of her children that this was a message from God to one of them.* There were seven of us that my mom had to warn, since my oldest brother was murdered a few years prior. At his funeral and in jail, I promised God I would surrender my life to Him. So, through those scriptures and warning, He was knocking on my heart for repentance and salvation to collect on my promises. When she called to share that message and warning, I knew immediately it was for me.

As years passed, Girl O and I were so saddened; because we then realized we were in a losing battle. We went through months of countless tears, distress, and loneliness as our relationship came to its end.

I decided to pack my things and check into a hotel room in California away Girl O and our friends. But before I left her home, our friends were calling to convince me to stay with her. They complimented our relationship and said things like: *your relationship is the ideal lesbian girls who they wanted to be like.* Then, *you two were meant for one another and you are making a big mistake.*

I laid on that hotel bed for hours pleading with God to: **"Save me, deliver me and set me free!"** People told me, *"Once gay, you will always be gay"*. I also asked God to: *save the female from my childhood experience, my college female lover, Girl A, Girl O; as well as women I had sexual involvements between these relationships.* Yearly, when I remember their birthdays or any of them come to mind, I continue to pray for them. I have a special place in my heart and in my prayer life for the homosexual community. They are loved; I love them, but God loved them first.

I especially asked God to heal Girl O and our broken hearts; because we truly believed our love for one another was eternally destined. The pain and hurt in my heart was almost unbearable. I needed God to rescue me from my enemy (which was "*inside of me*") and He did!

After I checked out of that hotel room, I moved back to Las Vegas because I felt God wanting me to reconcile my marriage. I called Jimmie to explain what was going on with me. I asked him could we give it another try and he accepted. He forgave me of all the wrong choices I made, things I did, and I forgave him. It took a while for our healing, wholeness and trusts to recover; but in time it was healed through the saving power of Jesus Christ!

Jimmie and I reconciled, and then remarried in Las Vegas for the third time. The next day after our marriage and because of the warning from God sent through my mother, I felt God leading me to go to church.

My issue with going to church was hearing teachings that made light of my kind of sinful struggles of homosexuality and sexual addictions. I would get very angry when I heard things like, "*God didn't make Adam and Steve, He made Adam and Eve*" then some of the congregation would laugh, "*Ha, ha, ha.*" There isn't anything funny about someone who struggles in their sexuality or any addiction. The church would openly welcome a recovering alcoholic, smoker, liar, thief, drug addict, etc. However, a recovering homosexual or sexually perverted person felt they had to hide, shut up and try to blend in. My sexual addiction to women, pornography, lying, cheating and so much more was a problem. **I was in need of a Savior to rescue me!**

Nevertheless, I was determined that nothing or no one would stop me from getting what I needed the most. I needed to be set free from the sins within me! God was so very tolerant with me and faithful to me. I love this scripture from 2 Peter 3:9 (AMP), which reads: "*The Lord does not delay and is not tardy or slow about what He promises, according to some people's conception of slowness, but He is long-suffering (extraordinarily patient) toward you, not desiring that any should perish, but that all should turn to repentance.*"

Therefore that sunny crisp Sunday morning of January 1997, I surrendered my body, heart, soul, spirit, and everything else I held onto and gave it all to God! I learned that I would continue to serve the master of sin if I did not surrender it all!

Two years after my salvation, Jimmie and I left Las Vegas and relocated to our hometown of Chicago. A few years later, Jimmie became very sick with congestive heart failure and emphysema which took his life. God blessed me to teach bible studies at home with Jimmie, pray with him and lead him into the arms of Jesus! Now he is in his resting place waiting on the Lord to rapture His people. Then God confirmed to me three times that Jimmie's soul was saved to enter into His heavenly home. Hallelujah!

Jimmie's death was a life changing occurrence for me, which life didn't prepare me for. Becoming a widow at 39 years old was not in the plan. At times, it was an emotional roller coaster. By the time he passed away, we were seriously in financial trouble. A few years prior, he made an agreement with a financial brokerage company to buy his lottery winnings and they paid him in a lump sum. With medical bills and our living expenses alone, we went through that money so fast. I was completely broke by then; I couldn't afford a headstone to put on his grave. Then to add salt to those wounds, three weeks after his death my job laid me off. During these painful years, I call this period: "*My Death Walk*", (which could be another book in itself). I journaled a lot, which became therapeutic; as the clock sometimes seemed to stand still. But through it all, God was my source of strength.

I am so very grateful that my parents took a firm stand in their beliefs of God's Word. They explained to me that homosexuality is against God's righteousness. They did not compromise their beliefs just because of their love for me. My parents treated my partners with respect and they received the same in return. They both have passed away, Mom in 2010 and Dad in 2011. I am truly grateful that I do not have to live with the guilt and pain that my parents loved me more than following God's will, way and His Holy Word. Now they are in their resting place with Jimmie and all of the other Believers waiting on their Savior to take them to their heavenly home!

In no way can I claim that temptation never visits me mentally or physically. There are many times that the devil would show me women who were my type, trying to enticement me. He would send demonic dreams, attacks and delusions trying to lure me back into sin, especially homosexuality. He tempted Jesus; therefore, I just signed up for his "*HIT LIST*" when I accepted Jesus Christ as my Lord and Savior. So, I must continually deny my desires and take up my cross daily (Luke 9:23) and follow Christ to fight my battles.

Since God has done so much for me, I wanted to serve Him any way that I could. He blessed me to start sharing with people everywhere about Him and leading them into a prayer of repentance to accept Him as their Lord and Savior. I later found out that this is a gift of "Evangelism" from Jesus. Then He allowed me to meet a wonderful couple who mentored me for years along with other ministers, to serve in prison ministry in Chicago Area County, Federal and State jails and prisons. Shortly afterward, God told my Pastor to ordain me in the office of an Evangelist.

After years of serving in jails and prisons, the Lord surprised me with another assignment.

I remember when Jimmie was still alive; we were attending church with my family in Chicago. The speaker that evening was a Prophetess visiting from Milwaukee, WI. She saw me in the hallway at church and said, *"God has another husband for you who's really going to love you very much."* I explained to her that after Jimmie, I never desired to marry again. Then, years later after Jimmie passed away, another Prophetess/Pastor was visiting at a different local church and she saw me in the church hallway and said, *"God has a husband for you and he's a Pastor."* Again, I explained to her that I was happily single as a widow and never desired to marry again. Then shared; *"I especially did not want to marry a Pastor."* Lastly, several years later at a prison ministry instructors' training, another Prophetess saw me in a hallway at that training conference and said, *"God has a husband for you and he's right around the corner."* I again had to explain, *"I never desired to marry again and no thank you."* But God!

As a result to my surprise, all of those Prophetesses were correct. The last Prophetess who told me that my husband was right around the corner was very accurate; he literally was in the next conference room around the corner. He was attending the same prison ministry instructors' training, as well. I only knew of him as a Senior Pastor of a church and a prison ministry volunteer. But, God had His timing in place.

One day I was at a maximum men's prison serving in ministry of sharing the gospel of Jesus Christ cell by cell. As I walked down the prison unit tier, God told Sr. Pastor Walter L. Poston to look down the tier and there I was, walking and talking with another volunteer. The following year he shared with me: *he was so frightened because at that very moment he felt love leap into his spirit!* He then left the building in fear. He felt fear because he was going through a divorce. He knew he needed time to receive the Lord's direction, restoration, forgiveness and strength before moving forward.

After much prayer and counselling, God's healing and restoration took place in Pastor Poston. After a short period of dating, we sought marriage counseling. We later started counseling with three marriage counselors, of which two are Pastors. Then, mid-spring of that year we were married in holy matrimony!

After a year of marriage and one visit to Las Vegas, NV, God told my husband that we were to move to Nevada (*Egypt to me*). I was frightened and not happy with this news. This is where the devil tried to kill, steal and destroy my purpose, destiny and calling. After fasting, praying and consecrating for ten weeks, God confirmed that this was His divine plan for us. Obediently, we resigned off of our jobs in 2009 as the recession peaked and drove seven states west to relocate to Las Vegas, Nevada. Finding ourselves homeless and totally depending on God's next directions was a total "**Faith Walk**".

Since our relocation to Las Vegas, God has blessed us and proven Himself in so many ways. We have met so many wonderful Believers who have been very generous to us. It is amazing how He opened wonderful doors of employment opportunities for us; when Las Vegas was ranked one of the highest unemployment cities during the recession in 2009. We met many individuals who lived in Las Vegas unemployed for years. But God brought us in and later blessed us tremendously because of our obedience.

We currently serve in six surrounding Las Vegas area men's, women's and youth jails and prisons. I never knew how large the Las Vegas penal system populations were until we started serving as volunteers in prison ministry. Now I see how God truly spared my life from years of incarceration.

The Lord is so awesome how He can use our misery for ministry. I am currently serving in the same County Jail where I was locked up. We are also serving in the women's prisons where I would have served almost 30 years of prison time if I had not repented and if God had not turned my life around.

So every time I go to minister into jails and prisons, I am reminded that I'm doing my prison time on my Gods' book and not for the devils'. Because satan sent evil for my destruction; now God is getting His glory, which He so well deserves!

There are so many more testimonies I could have included, so maybe those will be told in upcoming materials. Words can hardly express how God's grace has taken a broken heart with an empty soul and transformed it into His image! Now I see, "*THE PAIN THAT WAS IN MY PAST HAS BECOME THE PASSION BEHIND MY PURPOSE*", so now I can continually say: "**BUT GOD!**"

From my Heart to my Savior:

As Jesus' blood streamed down HIS body
with nails in His hands and feet,
Now I know that He did it all just for you and for me!
I kept hearing His voice but missed His point,
which would have been my life's disappoint.
Looking in a mirror, but couldn't see clearly who I was,
because sin's control had me so tight, I couldn't remember Christ's true love.
That empty void that hunted me for years,
has no more grip on me, and now it is all so clear.
Now I know I was created for much more than this,
because Jesus freed my heart and soul out of sin's horrible pits.
As I write this testimony of God's Love and Grace,
I sit at my desk as tears of gratitude stream down my face.
Now I'm free because of His unconditional Love,
a past adulteress, homosexual, and sinner -
that the devil and demons tried to trick and get rid of...

BUT GOD!

Facing the Facts –
Applying Truth for Relational Healing with God and Others

There is something about the word "TRUTH" that gives a since of assurance, liberty, and peace. According to the passage of St. John 8:32 (KJV) *"And ye shall know the truth, and the truth shall make you free"* brings validity to its promises.

1. WHAT IS RELATIONAL HEALING AND RELATIONAL WHOLENESS?

In scripture, God desires for His people to be healed and made whole (complete in Him). Jesus was falsely convicted to death, but through that conviction we are set free from the penalty of eternal separation from God. Through Jesus' punishment, He was beaten and from those whipped strips, we are healed and made whole. This healing can include: freedom from fear, habits, addictions, sickness and disease. As well as healing in relationships with family or friend, healing in our sexuality (the lack thereof, excessiveness, past violations and sexual identity), financial lack, and even healing from unbelief, just to name a few.

However, relational wholeness is taking your faith of healing to another level in Christ for spiritual fullness in Him. In other words, it is His keeping power and being set free from something or someone that had you bound. I like to say it in this fashion when I pray; *"The less of me and more of thee!"*

HEALING:
Psalm 103:2-4 (TLB)
² Yes, I will bless the Lord and not forget the glorious things he does for me.
³ He forgives all my sins. He heals me.
⁴ He ransoms me from hell. He surrounds me with loving-kindness and tender mercies.

Psalm 147:3 (KJV)
He healeth the broken in heart, and bindeth up their wounds.

Jeremiah 33:6 (KJV)
Behold, I will bring it health and cure, and I will cure them, and will reveal unto them the abundance of peace and truth.

Matthew 10:1 (KJV)
And when he had called unto him his twelve disciples, he gave them power against unclean spirits, to cast them out, and to heal all manner of sickness and all manner of disease.

James 5:15 (KJV)
And the prayer of faith shall save the sick, and the Lord shall raise him up; and if he have committed sins, they shall be forgiven him.

1 Peter 2:24 (KJV)
Who his own self bare our sins in his own body on the tree, that we, being dead to sins, should live unto righteousness: by whose stripes ye were healed.

WHOLENESS:
Matthew 11:28 (KJV)
Come unto me, all ye that labour and are heavy laden, and I will give you rest.

John 5:6 (KJV)
When Jesus saw him lie, and knew that he had been now a long time *in that case*, he saith unto him, Wilt thou be made whole?

Luke 17:19, Mark 5:34 & Mark 10:52 (KJV)
Jesus said: And he said unto him, Arise, go thy way: thy faith hath made thee whole.

Romans 5:3-4 (AMP)
[3] Moreover [let us also be full of joy now!] let us exult and triumph in our troubles and rejoice in our sufferings, knowing that pressure and affliction and hardship produce patient and unswerving endurance.
[4] And endurance (fortitude) develops maturity of character (approved faith and tried integrity). And character [of this sort] produces [the habit of joyful and confident hope of eternal salvation.

3 John 1:2 (KJV)
Beloved, I wish above all things that thou mayest prosper and be in health, even as thy soul prospereth.

2. WHAT IS SIN?

Sin is the act of being disobedient against God's will, way and Word (found in the Holy Bible). Another way to put it is *"to miss the mark."* Most individuals target is to make heaven their home. But, if that target isn't accomplished then they *"missed the mark."* Some synonyms are: to misfire, fail, end, defeat and slip.

Sin made each of us a sinner and this has made us wrongdoers, evildoers, offenders and criminals according to God's laws. Thankfully we have a way out of sin and through accepting God's way, which is to accept his gift of eternal life through Jesus Christ.

Proverbs 21:4 (TLB)
Pride, lust, and evil actions are all sin.

John 3:16 (KJV)
For God so loved the world, that he gave his only begotten Son, that whosoever believeth in him should not perish, but have everlasting life.

Romans 6:23 (KJV)
For the wages of sin is death; but the gift of God is eternal life through Jesus Christ our Lord.

James 4:17 (AMP)
So any person who knows what is right to do but does not do it, to him it is sin.

1 John 3:4 (AMP)
Everyone who commits (practices) sin is guilty of lawlessness; for [that is what] sin is, lawlessness (the breaking, violating of God's law by

transgression or neglect—being unrestrained and unregulated by His commands and His will).

3. WHAT DOES IT MEAN WHEN PEOPLE SAY "SIN SICK" (FOR EXAMPLE: WE LIVE IN A SIN-SICK WORLD)?

The meaning of sin is: being disobedient against God's will, way and Word. The sickness part of mankind is that we are born spiritually and morally corrupt. In other words, if we are spiritually and morally corrupt, then we are not well; which indicates we are not well or healthy due of sin. Synonyms for being sick are imperfect, infected, weak, unpleasant, helpless and being in a bad way.

When a person is sick they seek ways to get better. If they are unsuccessful in getting well, they will go to a physician, because he/she is a licensed professional who practice medicine for a cure. But the first step to recovery is to admit the sickness exists; because denial will make things worse with time. Throughout this book you will find additional scriptures to bring clarity to this meaning.

Romans 6:12-14 (NLT)
[12] Do not let sin control the way you live; do not give in to sinful desires.
[13] Do not let any part of your body become an instrument of evil to serve sin. Instead, give yourselves completely to God, for you were dead, but now you have new life. So use your whole body as an instrument to do what is right for the glory of God.

[14] Sin is no longer your master, for you no longer live under the requirements of the law. Instead, you live under the freedom of God's grace.

Romans 7:18-25 (NLT)
[18] And I know that nothing good lives in me, that is, in my sinful nature. I want to do what is right, but I can't.
[19] I want to do what is good, but I don't. I don't want to do what is wrong, but I do it anyway.
[20] But if I do what I don't want to do, I am not really the one doing wrong; it is sin living in me that does it.
[21] I have discovered this principle of life—that when I want to do what is right, I inevitably do what is wrong.
[22] I love God's law with all my heart.
[23] But there is another power within me that is at war with my mind. This power makes me a slave to the sin that is still within me.
[24] Oh, what a miserable person I am! Who will free me from this life that is dominated by sin and death?
[25] Thank God! The answer is in Jesus Christ our Lord. So you see how it is: In my mind I really want to obey God's law, but because of my sinful nature I am a slave to sin.

James 4:2-3 (NLT)
[2] You want what you don't have, so you scheme and kill to get it. You are jealous of what others have, but you can't get it, so you fight and wage war to take it away from them. Yet you don't have what you want because you don't ask God for it.

³ And even when you ask, you don't get it because your motives are all wrong--you want only what will give you pleasure.

4. DO YOU BELIEVE PEOPLE KNOW THEY ARE SINNING?

I believe individuals are aware of sin. God has given us a mechanism which we call our conscious (knowing right from wrong). I believe that's why people call my hometown, Las Vegas, "*Sin City*", it is because they are aware what sin is.

We know right from wrong through our spirit that God has given to each of us. This is how we connect and communicate with Him and each other (which is the ability to make choices in relationships, behaviors and decisions).

God is also a spirit and His nature is righteousness (*what's honorable, fair, good, holy, true, virtue and uncontaminated*). Any lifestyle or decision outside of God's nature violates the nature and character of God. Reading the Bible is a tool to use in finding who God is; but following His nature and character which is righteousness brings us in complete knowledge of knowing right from wrong.

For an example, when a person is enticed by lust (greed, envy, pornography, etc.) they go through behavioral changes. This indicates that they are aware that something is wrong. This behavior could lead to sins of lies, hatred, extra marital affairs, and so on to further fulfill this lust, which is sin.

Lastly, sin is so evil that we should seriously avoid it at any cost. Sin is as evil and wicked as God is holy and righteous; both are exceptionally contrary to one another!

Romans 1:18-22 (TLB)
[18] But God shows his anger from heaven against all sinful, evil men who push away the truth from them.
[19] For the truth about God is known to them instinctively; God has put this knowledge in their hearts.
[20] Since earliest times men have seen the earth and sky and all God made, and have known of his existence and great eternal power. So they will have no excuse when they stand before God at Judgment Day.
[21] Yes, they knew about him all right, but they wouldn't admit it or worship him or even thank him for all his daily care. And after a while they began to think up silly ideas of what God was like and what he wanted them to do. The result was that their foolish minds became dark and confused.
[22] Claiming themselves to be wise without God, they became utter fools instead.

Romans 3:23 (KJV)
For all have sinned, and come short of the glory of God;

Romans 6:1-4 (NLT)
[1] Well then, should we keep on sinning so that God can show us more and more of his wonderful grace?
[2] Of course not! Since we have died to sin, how can we continue to live in it?

³ Or have you forgotten that when we were joined with Christ Jesus in baptism, we joined him in his death?
⁴ For we died and were buried with Christ by baptism. And just as Christ was raised from the dead by the glorious power of the Father, now we also may live new lives.

1 Corinthians 10:13 (KJV)
There hath no temptation taken you but such as is common to man: but God is faithful, who will not suffer you to be tempted above that ye are able; but will with the temptation also make a way to escape, that ye may be able to bear it.

James 4:17 (AMP)
So any person who knows what is right to do but does not do it, to him it is sin.

1 John 3:8-9 (TLB)
⁸ But if you keep on sinning, it shows that you belong to Satan, who since he first began to sin has kept steadily at it. But the Son of God came to destroy these works of the devil.
⁹ The person who has been born into God's family does not make a practice of sinning because now God's life is in him; so he can't keep on sinning, for this new life has been born into him and controls him—he has been born again.

1 John 1:8 (KJV)
If we say that we have no sin, we deceive ourselves, and the truth is not in us.

5. How do you know the Bible is the real truth from God?

I know the Bible is the real truth from God because it has proven itself to me with confirmations. His Word helped free me from the bondage of the sin I lived in. Nothing else in life has given me this type of peace and fulfillment. It is the most sold and most controversial book in history. I haven't met or heard of anyone that could live by its precepts completely, but Jesus Christ. He confirmed that He came to fulfill the laws of it for an example to show us we can as well (Matthew 5:17).

Think about it, why would any person(s) make up these kinds of morals and values to live by when God give us free will? The Bible instructs us to love those who hate us, not to lie, steal, fornicate, commit adultery, murder unborn babies, etc. What individual would incorporate such instructions as these, but a Holy and righteous God?

Lastly, while I'm on this subject, be aware of antichrist. According to the Bible, anyone who is against Jesus Christ is an antichrist. These individuals persuade others not to believe the Bible is truth, spoken by God through mankind (also see: 1 John 2:18 and 2 John 1:7).

Mark 13:22 (KJV)
Jesus said: For false Christs and false prophets shall rise, and shall shew signs and wonders, to seduce, if it were possible, even the elect.

John 17:17 (KJV)
Jesus said: Sanctify them through thy truth: thy word is truth.

1 Timothy 2:3-4 (KJV)
³ For this is good and acceptable in the sight of God our Saviour;
⁴ Who will have all men to be saved, and to come unto the knowledge of the truth.

2 Timothy 3:16 (NLT)
All Scripture is inspired by God and is useful to teach us what is true and to make us realize what is wrong in our lives. It corrects us when we are wrong and teaches us to do what is right.

1 John 2:18 (TLB)
Dear children, this world's last hour has come. You have heard about the Antichrist who is coming—the one who is against Christ—and already many such persons have appeared. This makes us all the more certain that the end of the world is near.

1 John 4:1-3 (TLB)
¹Dearly loved friends, don't always believe everything you hear just because someone says it is a message from God: test it first to see if it really is. For there are many false teachers around,
² and the way to find out if their message is from the Holy Spirit is to ask: Does it really agree that Jesus Christ, God's Son, actually became man with a human body? If so, then the message is from God.
³ If not, the message is not from God but from one who is against Christ, like the "Antichrist" you have heard about who is going to come, and his attitude of enmity against Christ is already abroad in the world.

6. WHAT DOES IT MEAN TO FEAR GOD?

To fear God isn't to have terror, anxiety or be in distress like we would if we feared earthly things. However; the power in His holiness, His presence and His glory can be frightening to humanity.

To fear God's deity means <u>worshipping Him</u> (Proverbs 1:7 - loving on Him, spend time communicating in prayer talking to Him and listening to Him), <u>reverencing Him</u> (Psalm 1:2 - having respect for Him and being devoted to Him, spending time enjoyably reading and meditating on His Word), <u>loving Him</u> (Proverbs 8:13 - having an intimate "close and friendly" loving relationship with Him, hating what He hates and loving what He loves), <u>respecting Him</u> (Psalm 147:11 - having faith and hope in His Son, Jesus Christ), <u>obeying Him</u> (Psalm 111:10 - following His biblical instructions), and <u>submitting to Him</u> (Psalm 85:9 - surrendering your life).

To fear God brings wisdom, knowledge, joy, peace, love, blessings, and an abundant life!

Psalm 1:2 (KJV)
But his delight is in the law of the LORD; and in his law doth he meditate day and night.

Psalm 85:9 (KJV)
Surely his salvation *is* nigh them that fear him; that glory may dwell in our land.

Psalm 111:10 (KJV)
The fear of the Lord is the beginning of wisdom: a good understanding have all they that do his commandments: his praise endureth for ever.

Psalm 147:11 (KJV)
The Lord taketh pleasure in them that fear him, in those that hope in his mercy.

Proverbs 1:7 (KJV)
The fear of the Lord is the beginning of knowledge: but fools despise wisdom and instruction.

Proverbs 8:13 (KJV)
The fear of the Lord is to hate evil: pride, and arrogancy, and the evil way, and the froward mouth, do I hate.

2 Chronicles 7:14 (NLT)
Then if my people who are called by my name will humble themselves and pray and seek my face and turn from their wicked ways, I will hear from heaven and will forgive their sins and restore their land.

Matthew 10:28 and Luke 12:5 (KJV)
And fear not them which kill the body, but are not able to kill the soul: but rather fear him which is able to destroy both soul and body in hell.

7. WHY DO PEOPLE THINK THEY HAVE THE RIGHT TO JUDGE ME?

No one has the right to judge anyone else if God has not granted this permission. However, He has permitted this privilege to some of His leaders. He also allows our judicial system to have judges to keep order. Judging is determined when someone gives their opinion without true facts.

For example, the Prophet Nathan judged King David for his sins of committing adultery and murder. King David thought his sins were hidden from everyone but he and Bathsheba (2 Samuel 11th chapter and 2 Samuel 12:1-15).

Also, the Holy Spirit gives gifts to Christians, one of which is the gift of discerning of spirits (1 Corinthians 12:10). This gift allows a person to reveal truths from God; distinguish between right and wrong, good and evil, God's way or the devil's way. The Holy Spirit also was sent to judge those who do not follow God's righteousness and His coming judgment against sin.

We will all be judged by God and each of us must give an account for our own life to Him. Do not think people are judging you if they are simply showing you what God have said in His Holy Word. The Bible says, "'*Examine me, O LORD, and try me* (Psalm 26:2 - KJV),' '*But let a man examine himself* (1 Corinthians 11:28 - KJV),' '*Examine yourselves* (2 Corinthians 13:5 - KJV),' and '*Each one should test their own actions* (Galatians 6:4 – NIV,'" so this indicates God wants us to be our own judge alongside His Word for truth.

On the other hand, if you are confessing to be a Christian then this is how your lifestyle and actions should reflect. Being a Christian means to be *"Christ like."* It is a beautiful thing that God knows the intents of our hearts. However, the caution to that is God knows when we know right from wrong and simply refuse to follow what is right. The Bible reveals bitter and sweet messages to us and no one has the right to a 'la carte His Word to fit their own agenda.

Lastly, people are very opinionated. If the facts stacked against you has no validity, than ignore it. However, stay open to constructive criticism; it could help tremendously in the long run. Even King David had to encourage himself in the Lord (1 Samuel 30:6).

1 Samuel 16:7 (NLT)
But the LORD said to Samuel, "Don't judge by his appearance or height, for I have rejected him. The LORD doesn't see things the way you see them. People judge by outward appearance, but the LORD looks at the heart."

Psalm 96:13 (KJV)
Before the LORD: for he cometh, for he cometh to judge the earth: he shall judge the world with righteousness, and the people with his truth.

Matthew 7:1-2 (KJV)
[1] Judge not, that ye be not judged.
[2] For with what judgment ye judge, ye shall be judged: and with what measure ye mete, it shall be measured to you again.

John 16:7-11 (ASV)
[7] Nevertheless I tell you the truth: It is expedient for you that I go away; for if I go not away, the

Comforter will not come unto you; but if I go, I will send him unto you.
⁸ And he, when he is come, will convict the world in respect of sin, and of righteousness, and of judgment:
⁹ of sin, because they believe not on me;
¹⁰ of righteousness, because I go to the Father, and ye behold me no more;
¹¹ of judgment, because the prince of this world hath been judged.

Romans 14:10-12 (AMP)
¹⁰ Why do you criticize *and* pass judgment on your brother? Or you, why do you look down upon *or* despise your brother? For we shall all stand before the judgment seat of God.
¹¹ For it is written, As I live, says the Lord, every knee shall bow to Me, and every tongue shall confess to God [acknowledge Him to His honor and to His praise].
¹² And so each of us shall give an account of himself [give an answer in reference to judgment] to God.

Hebrews 12:6-8 &11 (AMP)
⁶ For the Lord corrects and disciplines everyone whom He loves, and He punishes, even scourges, every son whom He accepts and welcomes to His heart and cherishes.
⁷ You must submit to and endure [correction] for discipline; God is dealing with you as with sons. For what son is there whom his father does not [thus] train and correct and discipline?
⁸ Now if you are exempt from correction and left without discipline in which all [of God's children]

share, then you are illegitimate offspring and not true sons [at all].

¹¹ For the time being no discipline brings joy, but seems grievous and painful; but afterwards it yields a peaceable fruit of righteousness to those who have been trained by it [a harvest of fruit which consists in righteousness—in conformity to God's will in purpose, thought, and action, resulting in right living and right standing with God].

Hebrews 9:27 (KJV)
And as it is appointed unto men once to die, but after this the judgment:

1 Peter 4:17-18 (TLB)
¹⁷ For the time has come for judgment, and it must begin first among God's own children. And if even we who are Christians must be judged, what terrible fate awaits those who have never believed in the Lord?
¹⁸ If the righteous are barely saved, what chance will the godless have?

---

8. IF MY ABUSER ASKS FOR FORGIVENESS; HOW DO I ACCOMPLISH THIS WHEN I HAVE FEELINGS OF HATE FOR HIM/HER?

Forgiving that person will free you in so many ways. Your mind, body and soul will also receive healing and freedom it is longing for. Everyone wants to be and feel free. But, freedom is a choice. You may or may not agree, but you are in a good position when the abuser wants your forgiveness. Some people may tell you it is for his/her (the violator) own gain, but in reality it's best for all. Forgiveness will bring everyone involved freedom and God will bless you in return. On the other hand, holding on to the toxins of unforgiveness can cause mental and physical illnesses as well. Embrace this forgiveness, release the anger and/or pain and be set free.

> Proverbs 15:1 (KJV)
> A soft answer turneth away wrath: but grievous words stir up anger.
>
> Romans 12:17-18 (NIV)
> [17] Do not repay anyone evil for evil. Be careful to do what is right in the eyes of everyone.
> [18] If it is possible, as far as it depends on you, live at peace with everyone.
>
> Hebrews 10:30 (KJV)
> For we know him that hath said, Vengeance *belongeth* unto me, I will recompense, saith the Lord. And again, The Lord shall judge his people.
>
> Ephesians 4:32 (KJV)
> And be ye kind one to another, tenderhearted, forgiving one another, even as God for Christ's sake hath forgiven you.

Relational Matters – I'm at a Crossroad, Which Way Do I Go?

Using relational skills are not always the easiest task in life. Every aspect of these skills should be used very carefully. No matter how long we interact with humanity which includes ourselves, we will constantly see it's a never-ending assignment. Decisions…

9. CAN YOU EXPLAIN THE BODY, SOUL AND SPIRIT OF A HUMAN?

The Body: Is where we have 5 senses to function in this physical world; we hear (ear gate), see (eye gate), smell (nose gate), taste (mouth gate) and touch (feel gate).

I mentioned the gates here because this is how: either righteousness or sin gain access to our soul and spirit. This is where God, Jesus and the Holy Spirit desire to dwell to reveal holiness, righteousness and truth to us. However, we have an enemy who is satan and he desires access to bring lust, deception and ungodliness.

For examples, this is what satan brings:
To the BODY:
Ear Gate – listening to lies, conversations of dirty jokes, seductive music, etc. that will pollute the mind.

Eye Gate – looking at ungodly things or individuals with lustful desires (pornography) with the intent to eventually arouse the flesh.

Nose Gate – when you know a certain small is enticing, keep away from it (smell of alcohol or marijuana, his favorite cologne, her favorite perfume, etc.).

Mouth Gate – watching what we say about ourselves and others, because we can speak death or life to a situation.

Touch Gate – keeping our distance from touching, (things that belong to other) and being enticed to touch ungodly things (vices that lead to addictions) or individuals (person who is not our spouse or fighting).

The SOUL:
This is where we have the ability to make choices to have relationships within ourselves (self-worth), with others (those we love) and with God (faith in Him). This is also where the Holy Spirt dwells, who gives us a conscience and the will to make right choices in our behavior.

The SPIRIT:
This is where influences are controlled for our body and soul; as well as, our conscious and sub-conscious mind. This is where God has given us the privilege of free will.

It is through our spirit that we have communion and fellowship with God or satan. Our spirit also gives us intuition between good or evil, light or darkness, Holy or unholy, clean or unclean, and the choice to choose God's way or satan's way.

For an example, let's call this scenario "A Ticket."
- Your Body received "A Ticket" to eternity to live a life of truth from God or a life of lies from the devil.
- Your Spirit is in possession of the ticket to assure your final destination.
- Your Soul waits to enter heaven or hell from the ticket you obtained.

Matthew 16:26 (KJV)
For what is a man profited, if he shall gain the whole world, and lose his own soul? or what shall a man give in exchange for his soul?

Matthew 26:41 (KJV)
Watch and pray, that ye enter not into temptation: the spirit indeed is willing, but the flesh is weak.

John 4:24 (KJV)
God is a Spirit: and they that worship him must worship him in spirit and in truth.

Ephesian 4:22-24 (KJV)
^{22}That ye put off concerning the former conversation the old man, which is corrupt according to the deceitful lusts;
^{23} And be renewed in the spirit of your mind;
^{24} And that ye put on the new man, which after God is created in righteousness and true holiness.

Romans 7:21-25 (KJV)
^{21} I find then a law, that, when I would do good, evil is present with me.
^{22} For I delight in the law of God after the inward man:

²³ But I see another law in my members, warring against the law of my mind, and bringing me into captivity to the law of sin which is in my members.
²⁴ O wretched man that I am! who shall deliver me from the body of this death?
²⁵ I thank God through Jesus Christ our Lord. So then with the mind I myself serve the law of God; but with the flesh the law of sin.

1 Thessalonians 5:22-24 (KJV)
²² Abstain from all appearance of evil.
²³ And the very God of peace sanctify you wholly; and I pray God your whole spirit and soul and body be preserved blameless unto the coming of our Lord Jesus Christ.
²⁴ Faithful is he that calleth you, who also will do it.

10. THAT CHRISTIAN STUFF IS FOR OLD PEOPLE. WHY SHOULD I CARE ABOUT IT NOW? I'M YOUNG!

There are many youth and young kings in the Bible that served God, and He truly blessed them. Many young people mentioned in the Bible who did not obey Him (did things their way) had very little success or even died horrible deaths.

It is a blessing to serve God while you are young, because God has good things in store for everyone who obeys Him. (*I have personally met a number of young people that obeyed God, and they prospered in so many ways. A great number of these young individuals are doing well in school, some have wonderful jobs, lovely cars, nice apartments or homes and a few are married with beautiful children*). When we do things God's way, we receive God's results-which are always good. When we do things our way we receive our results which are usually not so good.

> Ecclesiastes 12:1 (NLT)
> Don't let the excitement of youth cause you to forget your Creator. Honor him in your youth before you grow old and say, "Life is not pleasant anymore."

> Psalm 119:9 (NIV)
> How can a young person stay on the path of purity? By living according to your word.

> 2 Kings 22:1-2 (NIV)
> [1] Josiah was eight years old when he became king, and he reigned in Jerusalem thirty-one years. His mother's name was Jedidah daughter of Adaiah; she was from Bozkath.
> [2] He did what was right in the eyes of the Lord and followed completely the ways of his father David, not turning aside to the right or to the left.

> 2 Kings 24:18 and 25:7 (NIV)
> [18] Zedekiah was twenty-one years old when he became king, and he reigned in Jerusalem eleven years. His mother's name was Hamutal daughter of Jeremiah; she was from Libnah.
> [25] They killed the sons of Zedekiah before his eyes. Then they put out his eyes, bound him with bronze shackles and took him to Babylon.

> 2 Chronicles 28:1 (NIV)
> Ahaz was twenty years old when he became king, and he reigned in Jerusalem sixteen years. Unlike

David his father, he did not do what was right in the eyes of the LORD.

2 Chronicles 29:1-2 (NIV)
¹ Hezekiah was twenty-five years old when he became king, and he reigned in Jerusalem twenty-nine years. His mother's name was Abijah daughter of Zechariah.
² He did what was right in the eyes of the LORD, just as his father David had done.

2 Chronicles 33:1-2 (NIV)
¹ Manasseh was twelve years old when he became king, and he reigned in Jerusalem fifty-five years.
² He did evil in the eyes of the LORD, following the detestable practices of the nations the LORD had driven out before the Israelites.

2 Chronicles 34:1-3 (NIV)
¹ Josiah was eight years old when he became king, and he reigned in Jerusalem thirty-one years.
² He did what was right in the eyes of the LORD and followed the ways of his father David, not turning aside to the right or to the left.
³ In the eighth year of his reign, while he was still young, he began to seek the God of his father David. In his twelfth year he began to purge Judah and Jerusalem of high places, Asherah poles and idols.

1 John 2:14-17 (TLB)
¹⁴ And so I say to you fathers who know the eternal God, and to you young men who are

strong with God's Word in your hearts, and have won your struggle against Satan:

[15] Stop loving this evil world and all that it offers you, for when you love these things you show that you do not really love God;

[16] for all these worldly things, these evil desires— the craze for sex, the ambition to buy everything that appeals to you, and the pride that comes from wealth and importance—these are not from God. They are from this evil world itself.

[17] And this world is fading away, and these evil, forbidden things will go with it, but whoever keeps doing the will of God will live forever.

11. "I WAS REALLY HURT BY PEOPLE AT THE LAST CHURCH, SO I JUST WATCH CHURCH ON TV. ISN'T THIS ENOUGH?"

As a Christian and a Pastor, please let me apologize for the hurt you experienced. There isn't any excuse for anyone to cause deliberate harm to anyone. I hope this person or persons involved had good intentions and meant no mistreatment. Sometime individuals have a dry sense of humor or their actions are misinterpreted. The bible states that: *Jesus is concerned about the least of us all* (Matthew 25:40).

We go to a church building to worship God as a unified body of Christ and this is where we should receive spiritual nourishment for our soul and spirit. When we are weak, we gain strength and knowledge from other strong Believers.

Please note; everyone that attends services at a church building isn't a Believer in Jesus Christ. The church building is like a hospital, this is where sin-sick people go to get spiritually well. Everyone in attendance may not be well, even if they serve in a ministry position. Besides, just because someone hurt you at one church do not mean it will happen at another one. I believe some things happen for better things to come.

Just a thought to ponder; have you ever been hurt by someone at work? Did you quit your job because of it? We must shake the dust from our shoes and stay focused. This is what Jesus instructed His disciples to do when they or their message wasn't received (Luke 9:5).

> Psalm 92:13 (KJV)
> Those that be planted in the house of the LORD shall flourish in the courts of our God.

> Psalm 133:1 (KJV)
> Behold, how good and how pleasant it is for brethren to dwell together in unity!

> Matthew 25:34-36 & 40 (KJV)
> [34] Then shall the King say unto them on his right hand, Come, ye blessed of my Father, inherit the kingdom prepared for you from the foundation of the world:
> [35] For I was an hungred, and ye gave me meat: I was thirsty, and ye gave me drink: I was a stranger, and ye took me in:
> [36] Naked, and ye clothed me: I was sick, and ye visited me: I was in prison, and ye came unto me.
>
> [40] And the King shall answer and say unto them, Verily I say unto you, Inasmuch as ye have done it unto one of the least of these my brethren, ye have done it unto me.

Hebrews 10:25 (NLT)
And let us not neglect our meeting together, as some people do, but encourage one another, especially now that the day of his return is drawing near.

12. WHAT ARE SOME EFFECTS FROM HAVING AN ABORTION AND HOW CAN I BE HEALED FROM THIS REGRET?

Many medical professionals have reported that internal and external abuses including addictions are linked to past abortion(s). Studies were established and revealed that the increase amounts of alcohol, prescription or street drugs addictions were high percentages for post-abortion women and men (even if his role was abandonment of the mother and the unborn child).

As trained counselors in an extremely busy prolife clinic, my husband and I counseled countless men and women clients. We found when proper counseling and therapy hasn't taken place, this experience can trigger unwanted episodes of depression, anxiety, nightmares, sexual dysfunction, roots of rejection, lack of trust, anger management issues, criminal behavior, promiscuous sexual behavior, lack of commitments, prostitution, pornography, multiple abortions and this list can continue. Some men experience delayed reactions which can be suppressed for years, but most women are affected immediately. Other factors can also hinder future relationships and/or marital problems even when the current partner had no involvement.

Also, this unfortunate experience is never far from the conscious of the abortionists. Two dates are always significant, the baby's birth date and the death date.

Yes, absolutely you can be healed from this regret. The power in Christ's blood will wash sickness, regrets and sorrows away, if you allow Him. His Love covers a multitude of sins.

Please know that your unborn baby is in the care of God. Your child loves you and has forgiven you. Anyone that is in the presence of the Lord has the heart of God and that is unconditional **LOVE**. Your child is "*In the presence of fullness of joy and pleasures forevermore*", according to Psalms 16:11. Began to ask God to forgive you and then ask your son or daughter in heaven for forgiveness as well.

If you have not had some kind of memorial service, consider planning one. Ask a trusted friend or family member to memorialize your baby's life with you. This memorial can help bring closure and be therapeutic. Remember, it is never too late to receive healing through the power of Jesus Christ. Ask Him and receive it.

> Psalm 27:10 (KJV)
> When my father and my mother forsake me, then the LORD will take me up.

> Psalm 127:3 (KJV)
> Lo, children are an heritage of the LORD: and the fruit of the womb is his reward.

> Isaiah 53:4-5 (KJV)
> [4] Surely he hath borne our griefs, and carried our sorrows: yet we did esteem him stricken, smitten of God, and afflicted.

⁵ But he was wounded for our transgressions, he was bruised for our iniquities: the chastisement of our peace was upon him; and with his stripes we are healed.

John 8:11 (KJV)
She said, No man, Lord. And Jesus said unto her, Neither do I condemn thee: go, and sin no more.

Romans 8:1 (KJV)
There is therefore now no condemnation to them which are in Christ Jesus, who walk not after the flesh, but after the Spirit.

2 Corinthians 5:8 (KJV)
We are confident, I say, and willing rather to be absent from the body, and to be present with the Lord.

13. HOW CAN AN INDIVIDUAL MOVE FORWARD WITH THEIR LIFE, WHEN THE SEXUAL PREDATOR DENIES HIS/HER ACTIONS OR HAS DIED?

If you desire to be healed and loosed from the power of the abuser, you must forgive. If you do not forgive, the individual will continue to have power in your life, even if they are in denial or deceased. Forgiveness is a crucial step toward freeing you from the roots of the abuse and the abuser. This may take some time, so be patient with yourself. Seek counseling or support groups; talking it out with someone else and not holding it inside will be a great support to lead you to wholeness and healing.

Psalm 34:18 (NIV)
The LORD is close to the brokenhearted and saves those who are crushed in spirit.

Proverbs 10:12 (KJV)
Hatred stirreth up strifes: but love covereth all sins.

Mark 11:25 (NIV)
And when you stand praying, if you hold anything against anyone, forgive them, so that your Father in heaven may forgive you your sins."

Galatians 6:7-8 (KJV)
[7] Be not deceived; God is not mocked: for whatsoever a man soweth, that shall he also reap.
[8] For he that soweth to his flesh shall of the flesh reap corruption; but he that soweth to the Spirit shall of the Spirit reap life everlasting.

14. WHAT ARE THE STEPS TO FORGIVENESS AND HEALING BEYOND MY SEXUAL ABUSE?

First and foremost, take it to the cross and let Jesus blood wash it away. Do not hold it in; get help through counseling, support groups and loved ones who are positive individuals. Your foundation should be faith in God's Word. Believe God can do it and receive His way of doing it. Then, changing your mindset of letting go of the past is freedom within itself. These are the beginning steps toward forgiveness and healing. Professionals in this area will have exercises and behavioral strategies to help direct your new path.

Psalm 56:8 (TLB)
You have seen me tossing and turning through the night. You have collected all my tears and preserved them in your bottle! You have recorded every one in your book.

Isaiah 41:10 (KJV)
Fear thou not; for I am with thee: be not dismayed; for I am thy God: I will strengthen thee; yea, I will help thee; yea, I will uphold thee with the right hand of my righteousness.

Isaiah 53:5 (KJV)
But he *was* wounded for our transgressions, *he was* bruised for our iniquities: the chastisement of our peace *was* upon him; and with his stripes we are healed.

Matthew 6:14-15 (AMP)
14 For if you forgive people their trespasses [their reckless and willful sins, leaving them, letting them go, and giving up resentment], your heavenly Father will also forgive you.
15 But if you do not forgive others their trespasses [their reckless and willful sins, leaving them, letting them go, and giving up resentment], neither will your Father forgive you your trespasses.

Ephesians 4:32 (KJV)
And be ye kind one to another, tenderhearted, forgiving one another, even as God for Christ's sake hath forgiven you.

15. IS IT NECESSARY FOR AN INDIVIDUAL TO ASK GOD TO FORGIVE HIM, WHEN HE WAS THE VICTIM OF ABUSE?

Everyone has sinned, so we all must ask for forgiveness. When human nature is damaged by the devil's control through an individual to harm someone physically, mentally or emotionally, that pain and scar is real. Therefore, when someone is victimized they usually start to build hatred and resentment toward the abuser. If this has happened, then ask God for forgiveness of what has built up in your heart. By doing this cleansing, it will help free you from the power of the abuser. This is also the beginning process for freedom to receive healing and wholeness in your mind, body and soul.

I recently had someone deliberately wrong me several times; I could not let their actions bring hatred in my heart. I had to pray and follow God's Word as Jeremiah 31:3 says, *"Therefore with lovingkindness have I drawn thee."* I had to continue treating her with the love of Christ and this gave her a change of heart toward me. She began to respect me in return and later blessed me financially. By doing this, it will stop further infectious germs (anger, resentment, hated, pain, etc.) to fester and it will bring healing to the pain and scars you endured.

Mark 11:25-26 (AMP)
[25] And whenever you stand praying, if you have anything against anyone, forgive him and let it drop (leave it, let it go), in order that your Father Who is in heaven may also forgive you your [own] failings and shortcomings and let them drop.

²⁶ But if you do not forgive, neither will your Father in heaven forgive your failings and shortcomings.

Romans 3:23 (KJV)
For all have sinned, and come short of the glory of God;

Ephesians 4:31-32 (KJV)
³¹ Let all bitterness, and wrath, and anger, and clamour, and evil speaking, be put away from you, with all malice:
³² And be ye kind one to another, tenderhearted, forgiving one another, even as God for Christ's sake hath forgiven you.

16. WHEN IS IT A GOOD TIME TO CONFRONT THE ONE WHO VIOLATED YOU?

There's no one-fit-all answer to this question. Confronting an unhealthy individual isn't the easiest thing to do. When the abused person has received their healing, this may be the most suitable time. Seek spiritual and medical counsel; then be led by the Holy Spirit. When a person's soul has been wounded there is too much pain embedded. Only God who created your soul can heal it and make it whole again.

Proverbs 3:5-6 (KJV)
⁵ Trust in the Lord with all thine heart; and lean not unto thine own understanding.
⁶ In all thy ways acknowledge him, and he shall direct thy paths.

Proverbs 15:22 (KJV)
Without counsel purposes are disappointed: but in the multitude of counsellers they are established.

Romans 12:17-19 (NIV)
[17] Do not repay anyone evil for evil. Be careful to do what is right in the eyes of everyone.
[18] If it is possible, as far as it depends on you, live at peace with everyone.
[19] Do not take revenge, my dear friends, but leave room for God's wrath, for it is written: "It is mine to avenge; I will repay," says the Lord.

17. IS PREMARITAL COUNSELING NECESSARY?

Absolutely! Overtime, premarital counseling saves marriages and is not predominately for times when problems arise. Premarital counseling is a preservative; it stabilizes marriage in difficult times before situations escalate. This is the time to discuss those hard to talk about issues, while everyone is pleasant. At a minimum, these few examples should be discussed among the two of you:

- Are we going to have children? When, how many?
- Can my mom live with us for a little while since my dad has recently passed away? How long?
- Frequently, my family borrows money from me, is this okay?
- Can my adult children live with us if they fall on hard times? How long?
- I coach little league teams during baseball season, would this be a problem?

The divorce rate is so high because too often people plan and plan again for that perfect wedding day and never took time to plan for the marriage. Marriage should be life-long, *"from this day forward until death do us part."*

I sure wish someone had given me this advice in my first marriage. It probably would have saved my late husband and me a lot of heartaches. Therefore, my current husband and I had three marriage counselors, two of whom are Pastors.

There are many facets of life that have already taken place with the two individuals planning to marry. It is really unfair to one another not to at least discuss some of these situations with a marriage counselor. Love feels good when everything is going well and at the dating and honeymoon phase.

Communication is the key to a successful marriage. This could be devastating and even overwhelming to find out what will affect the other person if things are not discussed prior to saying; *"I Do."*

I listed a few additional questions to ponder (8 categories; because 8 is the number of *New Beginnings*):

1. Why me - Why do you want to marry me? Do I have similarities of any of your past companions?
2. Our responsibilities to one another - How does scripture instruct me as becoming a husband or a wife? What are your Christian beliefs concerning us as a couple and for our family?
3. Family - How would you discipline my children? Will we raise our children with Christian values?

4. <u>Past relationships</u> - Have you let go of soul ties from previous relationships? How, when, etc.
5. <u>Past experiences</u> - Have you had or been involved in a relationship that an abortion occurred? (Please read the question and answer of number 12 in this book why this is very important).
6. <u>Sexual experiences</u> - Have your ever had a homosexual experience or attraction?
7. <u>Health</u> – If you are not a virgin, when was your last HIV/AIDS test? What were the results? Should we take a test prior to us getting married?
8. <u>Finances</u> - How is your credit rating and what financial debt do you owe? Do you have any past or present bankruptcies, judgments or lawsuits against you? (Finances are major issues which caused many divorces).

Proverbs 11:14 (KJV)
Where no counsel is, the people fall: but in the multitude of counsellors there is safety.

Proverbs 18:22 (NLT)
The man who finds a wife finds a treasure, and he receives favor from the Lord.

Proverbs 12:15 (AMP)
The way of a fool is right in his own eyes, but he who listens to counsel is wise.

1 Corinthians 7:2-5 (ASV)
[2] But, because of fornications, let each man have his own wife, and let each woman have her own husband.

³ Let the husband render unto the wife her due: and likewise also the wife unto the husband.
⁴ The wife hath not power over her own body, but the husband: and likewise also the husband hath not power over his own body, but the wife.
⁵ Defraud ye not one the other, except it be by consent for a season, that ye may give yourselves unto prayer, and may be together again, that Satan tempt you not because of your incontinency.

Ephesians 5:21-31 (KJV)
²¹ Submitting yourselves one to another in the fear of God.
²² Wives, submit yourselves unto your own husbands, as unto the Lord.
²³ For the husband is the head of the wife, even as Christ is the head of the church: and he is the saviour of the body.
²⁴ Therefore as the church is subject unto Christ, so let the wives be to their own husbands in everything.
²⁵ Husbands, love your wives, even as Christ also loved the church, and gave himself for it;
²⁶ That he might sanctify and cleanse it with the washing of water by the word,
²⁷ That he might present it to himself a glorious church, not having spot, or wrinkle, or any such thing; but that it should be holy and without blemish.
²⁸ So ought men to love their wives as their own bodies. He that loveth his wife loveth himself.
²⁹ For no man ever yet hated his own flesh; but nourisheth and cherisheth it, even as the Lord the church:

³⁰ For we are members of his body, of his flesh, and of his bones.
³¹ For this cause shall a man leave his father and mother, and shall be joined unto his wife, and they two shall be one flesh.

18. IS IT OKAY TO BE HAPPILY UNMARRIED?

There is nothing wrong or strange about not wanting to be married.

The Apostle Paul said, "*It was better for the unmarried and for widows to remain unmarried.*" I believe he said this for a variety of reasons to show the freedom of having time in doing the Lord's work. Jesus showed this to be true as well. They had fewer distractions to do the assignments God sent them on earth to complete.

Let us look at a synonym of each word pointed out in the amplified version of 1 Corinthians 7:8, which describes it is "*well*" to stay unmarried; *good* (virtuous), *advantageous* (beneficial), *expedient* (useful), and *wholesome* (good). Therefore, if this is the will of God for you to stay unmarried for freedom to serve Him; then you have been chosen for an honorable, favorable, valuable and respectable assignment from God!

> Isaiah 54:5 (KJV)
> For thy Maker is thine husband; the Lord of hosts is his name; and thy Redeemer the Holy One of Israel; The God of the whole earth shall he be called.

Matthew 19:12 (AMP)
For there are eunuchs who have been born incapable of marriage; and there are eunuchs who have been made so by men; and there are eunuchs who have made themselves incapable of marriage for the sake of the kingdom of heaven. Let him who is able to accept this accept it.

1 Corinthians 7:7-8 (AMP)
^{7} I wish that all men were like I myself am [in this matter of self-control]. But each has his own special gift from God, one of this kind and one of another.
^{8} But to the unmarried people and to the widows, I declare that it is well (good, advantageous, expedient, and wholesome) for them to remain [single] even as I do.

1 Corinthians 7:32-40 (NIV)
^{32} In all you do, I want you to be free from worry. An unmarried man can spend his time doing the Lord's work and thinking how to please him.
^{33} But a married man can't do that so well; he has to think about his earthly responsibilities and how to please his wife.
^{34} His interests are divided. It is the same with a girl who marries. She faces the same problem. A girl who is not married is anxious to please the Lord in all she is and does. But a married woman must consider other things such as housekeeping and the likes and dislikes of her husband.
^{35} I am saying this to help you, not to try to keep you from marrying. I want you to do whatever will help you serve the Lord best, with as few other things as possible to distract your attention from him.

³⁶ But if anyone feels he ought to marry because he has trouble controlling his passions, it is all right; it is not a sin; let him marry.
³⁷ But if a man has the willpower not to marry and decides that he doesn't need to and won't, he has made a wise decision.
³⁸ So the person who marries does well, and the person who doesn't marry does even better.
³⁹ The wife is part of her husband as long as he lives; if her husband dies, then she may marry again, but only if she marries a Christian.
⁴⁰ But in my opinion she will be happier if she doesn't marry again; and I think I am giving you counsel from God's Spirit when I say this.

19. SHOULD AN EX-GAY PERSON SEEK TO BE IN A HETEROSEXUAL MARRIAGE TO KEEP THEM STRAIGHT?

Getting married to the opposite gender will not cure same-sex cravings nor is it a solution to be heterosexual. I would suggest working on yourself and your spiritual growth first. Submitting to Godly council with mentorship before making this decision is important. Then, give yourself time to process your new life before making a lifelong marriage commitment.

In time, seek a spouse only if you believe that this is the will of God for you. Marriage according to the will of God is a wonderful union and brings many blessings when it is done His way.

Philippians 4:11 (AMP)
Not that I am implying that I was in any personal want, for I have learned how to be content (satisfied to the point where I am not disturbed or disquieted) in whatever state I am.

Philippians 4:13 (KJV)
I can do all things through Christ which strengtheneth me.

1 Corinthians 7:2 (KJV)
Nevertheless, to avoid fornication, let every man have his own wife, and let every woman have her own husband.

20. MY SON IS GAY AND I LOVE HIM DEARLY, BUT I DO NOT AGREE WITH HIS CHOICE OF LIFESTYLE, WHAT SHOULD I DO?

The key is that you love your child genuinely. Loving your child is priceless in itself. When children are young they receive the necessities in life along with parental guidance. However, when they become adults, they must have the freedom of choice. If he loves you in return, he will respect your decision as well as you respecting his decisions; even if you're not in agreement. Nonetheless, you can love without compromise.

Find healing scriptures and insert your son's name in it, then pray those scriptures to God for results. For an example: Jeremiah 33:6 (KJV) Behold, I will bring (John) it health and cure, and I will cure (John) them, and will reveal unto (John) them the abundance of peace and truth.

You must be patient; God's timing isn't like our timing. Jesus shared that prayer and fasting brings deliverances. I am a living testimony that this works!

Jeremiah 31:3b (KJV)
Yea, I have loved thee with an everlasting love: therefore with lovingkindness have I drawn thee.

Matthew 10:37 (KJV)
Jesus said: He that loveth father or mother more than me is not worthy of me: and he that loveth son or daughter more than me is not worthy of me.

Mark 10:29-30 (TLB)
[29] And Jesus replied, "Let me assure you that no one has ever given up anything—home, brothers, sisters, mother, father, children, or property—for love of me and to tell others the Good News,
[30] who won't be given back, a hundred times over, homes, brothers, sisters, mothers, children, and land—with persecutions! "All these will be his here on earth, and in the world to come he shall have eternal life.

Matthew 17:21 also Mark 9:29 (KJV)
Jesus said: And he said unto them, This kind can come forth by nothing, but by prayer and fasting.

21. MY DAUGHTER DESIRES TO BRING HER LESBIAN PARTNER TO THANKSGIVING DINNER, SHOULD I ALLOW THIS?

If your daughter and her partner is an adult, then treat her as an adult guest in your home. If she is a minor, I believe you should not allow it. God requires parents to teach their children His morals and values. That's why children are called adolescents, I heard someone say: *"because they are absent of adult life lessons."*

On the other hand, ask your adult child to explain to her partner to respect your home and your Christian values. Also, that any activity outside of God's order is not allowed in your home (hugging, kissing, touching one another, etc.). This should be honored for any unmarried heterosexual couples as well, because God isn't a respecter of persons. Show them the love of Jesus, plant a loving seed and leave the results to God.

> Jeremiah 31:3b (KJV)
> Yea, I have loved thee with an everlasting love: therefore with lovingkindness have I drawn thee.
>
> Acts 10:34 also Romans 2:11 (NLT)
> Then Peter replied, "I see very clearly that God shows no favoritism.
>
> Matthew 5:46-47 (NIV)
> [46] If you love those who love you, what reward will you get? Are not even the tax collectors doing that?

⁴⁷ And if you greet only your own people, what are you doing more than others? Do not even pagans do that?

Mark 2:15-17 (NIV)
¹⁵ While Jesus was having dinner at Levi's house, many tax collectors and sinners were eating with him and his disciples, for there were many who followed him.
¹⁶ When the teachers of the law who were Pharisees saw him eating with the sinners and tax collectors, they asked his disciples: "Why does he eat with tax collectors and sinners?"
¹⁷ On hearing this, Jesus said to them, "It is not the healthy who need a doctor, but the sick. I have not come to call the righteous, but sinners."

22. MY DAUGHTER WANTS TO RAISE MY GRANDDAUGHTER IN HER HOME WITH HER LESBIAN LOVER, SHOULD I ALLOW THIS?

If your daughter is an adult, let her be an adult to raise her own child. You may be at odds about this arrangement, but ask God for wisdom. However, being a supportive parent as much as possible will be comforting to her of your love. Continue to pray for the safety and well-being of all involved. Let the Lord guide her out of this arrangement and try not to interfere. Love and patience with perseverance is the key.

Please review the prayer exercise in question number 20 in this book for ways to pray for your daughter & granddaughter. Find additional scriptures that will bring salvation, love and unity for your family.

Isaiah 40:31 (KJV)
But they that wait upon the Lord shall renew their strength; they shall mount up with wings as eagles; they shall run, and not be weary; and they shall walk, and not faint.

Romans 15:4-6 (KJV)
4 For whatsoever things were written aforetime were written for our learning, that we through patience and comfort of the scriptures might have hope.
5 Now the God of patience and consolation grant you to be likeminded one toward another according to Christ Jesus:
6 That ye may with one mind and one mouth glorify God, even the Father of our Lord Jesus Christ.

1 Corinthians 16:14 (ASV)
Let all that ye do be done in love.

James 1:2-5 (NIV)
2 Consider it pure joy, my brothers and sisters, whenever you face trials of many kinds,
3 because you know that the testing of your faith produces perseverance.
4 Let perseverance finish its work so that you may be mature and complete, not lacking anything.
5 If any of you lacks wisdom, you should ask God, who gives generously to all without finding fault, and it will be given to you.

23. MY FAMILY DISOWNED ME SINCE I ACCEPTED JESUS AND WOULD NOT ACCEPT MY MOM'S LESBIAN LIFESTYLE. WHAT SHOULD I DO?

Defiantly pray for them and show them the love of Jesus. Your mom is an adult and her choice of lifestyle is her decision, which no one can change but God. Respect and love her as your mother; then assure her that your love for her hasn't changed. This should free the rest of your family from their resentments toward you.

We did not choose who would be our natural family members, so trust God for their salvation. God had a reason He put you with the family you are in and maybe it is to win their souls to Christ. The best message a person can relate is showing the love of Jesus through their own lifestyle.

The beauty of accepting Jesus as our Savior; we receive a new family in the Lord. We are adopted into God's royal family as His child and become a part of His huge family with other Believers!

> Psalm 27:10 (KJV)
> When my father and my mother forsake me, then the LORD will take me up.

> Proverbs 16:7 (KJV)
> When a man's ways please the LORD, he maketh even his enemies to be at peace with him.

> Matthew 4:22 (KJV)
> And they immediately left the ship and their father, and followed him.

Matthew 12:46-50 also see Mark 3:31-35 (KJV)
46 While he yet talked to the people, behold, his mother and his brethren stood without, desiring to speak with him.
47 Then one said unto him, Behold, thy mother and thy brethren stand without, desiring to speak with thee.
48 But he answered and said unto him that told him, Who is my mother? and who are my brethren?
49 And he stretched forth his hand toward his disciples, and said, Behold my mother and my brethren!
50 For whosoever shall do the will of my Father which is in heaven, the same is my brother, and sister, and mother.

Matthew 19:29 (KJV)
Jesus said: And every one that hath forsaken houses, or brethren, or sisters, or father, or mother, or wife, or children, or lands, for my name's sake, shall receive an hundredfold, and shall inherit everlasting life.

Luke 12:51-53 (ASV)
Jesus said: 51 Think ye that I am come to give peace in the earth? I tell you, Nay; but rather division:
52 for there shall be from henceforth five in one house divided, three against two, and two against three.
53 They shall be divided, father against son, and son against father; mother against daughter, and daughter against her mother; mother in law against her daughter in law, and daughter in law against her mother in law.

Romans 8:14-17 (KJV)
[14] For as many as are led by the Spirit of God, they are the sons of God.
[15] For ye have not received the spirit of bondage again to fear; but ye have received the Spirit of adoption, whereby we cry, Abba, Father.
[16] The Spirit itself beareth witness with our spirit, that we are the children of God:
[17] And if children, then heirs; heirs of God, and joint-heirs with Christ; if so be that we suffer with him, that we may be also glorified together.

Homosexuality - "Help" I'm having An Identity Crises

Same-sex attraction is on the rise and individuals need to know the truth about their identity. God uniquely made each of us male or female. He even gave hermaphrodites (infants born with both male and female sexual organs) individuality to be a male or female. Outside of these God giving identities, people have created so many labels for homosexual lifestyles that it is almost impossible to keep up. These are a few examples:

- Androsexual
- Asexual
- Bigender
- Bisexual
- Butch
- Cisgender
- Demi Sexual
- Down-low
- Drag King
- Drag Queen
- Dyke
- En Femme
- Faggot
- Femme
- Family
- Gay
- Genderless
- Genderqueer
- Intersex
- Intergender
- Lipstix Lesbian
- Pansexual
- Same Gender Loving (SGL)
- Skoliosexual
- Transgender
- Trans-man
- Trans-woman
- Third Gender
- Transsexual
- Transvestite
- Queer
- Metrosexual
- Multi-Gendered
- Multisexual
- Polysexual
- Punk
- Sissy
- Trade (T')

And there are many more. Individuals who created these labels have caused **"An Identity Crises"**; especially for our youth as well as the matured! Please do not allow people to put labels on you. Satan has done this for decades, now so many individuals are living with its scars. Such as parents calling their children: "stupid", "dumb", "you're like your no good daddy", then society: "you're not good enough", "fatty", "skinny", "too short", "too tall", etc.

We have one Creator and He has uniquely customized each of us the way He intended.

24. ARE PEOPLE BORN HOMOSEXUAL?

The "born homosexual" agenda practically has no biblical truth in itself or firm scientific conclusions. This theory has kept individuals confused and burden for way too long. However, all mankind has inherited a sin nature; therefore the "born homosexual" agenda has no validity over any other sin. To be honest, this is the excuse so many people have used to validate their decision to remain in this lifestyle and behavior.

I do not claim to be an expert on this subject but, God made each of us to be male and female, which is who we are first and foremost. The born homosexuality term would make a person a third gender and God only made two. If a person was born homosexual that would mean he or she has no way out and why would God create us to condemn us? And if He did, He would need to repent to humanity and especially to the people of Sodom and Gomorrah, even people in Noah's days for destroying them because of their choices of living in sin.

When a person chooses to live as a homosexual, this choice still doesn't change nature. As a result, when a very masculine lesbian chooses to live as a male, that decision doesn't stop her monthly cycle from naturally taking course. Or even a very feminine male, his mustache and beard will still grow. We cannot change who God created us to be, but it can be altered through medications and surgical procedures to fit our choice of lifestyles.

Anyone who sincerely surrenders their will to God for freedom from its strongholds has the right to be free or any other sin through the power of Jesus Christ. When Jesus came to earth in human flesh He did not fight satan with His human nature, He fought satan with the Word of God.

God is very mindful of His human creations. He gave us His best and wants the best for us. According to Psalms 8:4-6 and Hebrews 2:6-9, God has positioned mankind a little lower than His angels; then purposed us to be sovereigns in His created order. Therefore, He made no mistake when He made us male and female.

> Genesis 1:27 (KJV)
> So God created man in his own image, in the image of God created he him; male and female created he them.

Genesis 2:22-24 (KJV)
[22] And the rib, which the Lord God had taken from man, made he a woman, and brought her unto the man.
[23] And Adam said, This is now bone of my bones, and flesh of my flesh: she shall be called Woman, because she was taken out of Man.
[24] Therefore shall a man leave his father and his mother, and shall cleave unto his wife: and they shall be one flesh.

Psalm 51:5 (NIV)
Surely I was sinful at birth, sinful from the time my mother conceived me.

Matthew 19:4 also Mark 10:6 (KJV)
And he answered and said unto them, Have ye not read, that he which made them at the beginning made them male and female,

John 8:32 (KJV)
And ye shall know the truth, and the truth shall make you free.

Romans 1:24-32 (TLB)
[24] So God let them go ahead into every sort of sex sin, and do whatever they wanted to—yes, vile and sinful things with each other's bodies.
[25] Instead of believing what they knew was the truth about God, they deliberately chose to believe lies. So they prayed to the things God made, but wouldn't obey the blessed God who made these things.
[26] That is why God let go of them and let them do all these evil things, so that even their women

turned against God's natural plan for them and indulged in sex sin with each other.

²⁷ And the men, instead of having normal sex relationships with women, burned with lust for each other, men doing shameful things with other men and, as a result, getting paid within their own souls with the penalty they so richly deserved.

²⁸ So it was that when they gave God up and would not even acknowledge him, God gave them up to doing everything their evil minds could think of.

²⁹ Their lives became full of every kind of wickedness and sin, of greed and hate, envy, murder, fighting, lying, bitterness, and gossip.

³⁰ They were backbiters, haters of God, insolent, proud, braggarts, always thinking of new ways of sinning and continually being disobedient to their parents.

³¹ They tried to misunderstand, broke their promises, and were heartless—without pity.

³² They were fully aware of God's death penalty for these crimes, yet they went right ahead and did them anyway and encouraged others to do them, too.

25. WHAT CAUSES A PERSON TO BE ATTRACTED TO THE SAME GENDER?

It could be a number of reasons that causes a person to be attracted to the same gender. The root could be a lack of love, perceived or real. The list is unmeasurable.

First and foremost, being attracted to the same gender is a sinful desire that satan brings to lure an individual into sin. It is the same tactic he used at the beginning of time to entice Eve into sin. The root starts through our power to resist or surrender to sin. Through the Bible, we learn that evil spirits gain access through demonic spirits. This happens when they find an entry way.

It all starts in the spirit realm. We are human spirits, housed in a fleshly and sinful body. Our choices feed our destiny until we decide to change its course.

<u>This is the lie Eve believed from satan:</u>
Genesis 3:2-5 (ASV)
² And the woman said unto the serpent, Of the fruit of the trees of the garden we may eat:
³ but of the fruit of the tree which is in the midst of the garden, God hath said, Ye shall not eat of it, neither shall ye touch it, lest ye die.
⁴ And the serpent said unto the woman, Ye shall not surely die:
⁵ for God doth know that in the day ye eat thereof, then your eyes shall be opened, and ye shall be as God, knowing good and evil.

Proverbs 14:12 & 16:25 (KJV)
There is a way which seemeth right unto a man, but the end thereof are the ways of death.

John 10:10 (KJV)
Jesus said: The thief cometh not, but for to steal, and to kill, and to destroy: I am come that they might have life, and that they might have it more abundantly.

26. WHY IS THE HOMOSEXUAL LIFESTYLE BELIEVED TO BE A MATTER OF CHOICE?

It is not just the homosexual lifestyle being a matter of choice; we are all born into sin and by nature everyone has sinned.

Individuals choose this lifestyle because of deception. They believe the lie of satan that it is not him that is making them chose this behavior, and he tells them that there is no way to be healed, delivered and set free. We overcome deception by coming into the knowledge of truth and that's who Jesus is; He's the Way, the Truth and the Life! The devil has lied since the beginning of time, and he's yet in the lying business today.

Be it homosexuality, murder, lying and the list goes on... In scripture, 1 John 3:15, it tells us that *"hatred is murder,"* most people do not act fully upon this sin/crime because they know the consequences from the laws which is years in prison or even losing their life. Even some lies for an example: filing false police reports, purchasing firearms, lying on tax returns, etc. are stiff penalties according to the law. These penalties keep individual's from lying. So yes, these examples shows it is a matter of choice in our behavior which sin we chose to continue to live in. Homosexuality or any sexual relations outside of holy matrimony is clearly sexual disobedience against God's righteousness.

God so beautifully gave us choices and free will. Therefore, we should honor Him with this privilege and willingly choose to follow His way.

Joshua 24:15 (KJV)
And if it seem evil unto you to serve the LORD, choose you this day whom ye will serve; whether the gods which your fathers served that *were* on the other side of the flood, or the gods of the Amorites, in whose land ye dwell: but as for me and my house, we will serve the LORD.

Romans 5:12 (AMP)
Therefore, as sin came into the world through one man, and death as the result of sin, so death spread to all men, [no one being able to stop it or to escape its power] because all men sinned.

1 Thessalonians 4:7-8 (TLB)
[7] For God has not called us to be dirty-minded and full of lust but to be holy and clean.
[8] If anyone refuses to live by these rules, he is not disobeying the rules of men but of God who gives his Holy Spirit to you.

James 1:13-15 (NLT)
[13] And remember, when you are being tempted, do not say, "God is tempting me." God is never tempted to do wrong, and he never tempts anyone else.
[14] Temptation comes from our own desires, which entice us and drag us away.
[15] These desires give birth to sinful actions. And when sin is allowed to grow, it gives birth to death.

27. IS HOMOSEXUALITY THE WORST SIN IN THE BIBLE?

Absolutely not. Homosexuality isn't the worst sin in the bible; however Jesus mentioned in St. John 19:11 there is a greater sin. Yet, it does mention in several passages that homosexuality is an abominable sin (terrible, awful, horrible, offensive and detestable).

All sin is against God and He will judge all unrepented sin. All sin will equal the punishment of being eternally separated from God and hell's fire will fit the penalty of sin itself. However, 1 John 1:9 declares: *"If we confess our sins, God will forgive us of our sins"*. Jesus warns us that blasphemy (to curse or swear) against the Holy Ghost shall not be forgiven.

> John 19:11 (NIV)
> Jesus answered, "You would have no power over me if it were not given to you from above. Therefore the one who handed me over to you is guilty of a greater sin."

> Matthew 12:31-32 also Mark 3:28-30 (KJV)
> [31] Wherefore I say unto you, All manner of sin and blasphemy shall be forgiven unto men: but the blasphemy against the Holy Ghost shall not be forgiven unto men.
> [32] And whosoever speaketh a word against the Son of man, it shall be forgiven him: but whosoever speaketh against the Holy Ghost, it shall not be forgiven him, neither in this world, neither in the world to come.

Leviticus 18:22
(KJV) Thou shalt not lie with mankind, as with womankind: it is abomination
Again -
(NLT) "Do not practice homosexuality, having sex with another man as with a woman. It is a detestable sin.

Leviticus 20:13
(KJV) If a man also lie with mankind, as he lieth with a woman, both of them have committed an abomination: they shall surely be put to death; their blood shall be upon them.
Again -
(NLT) "If a man practices homosexuality, having sex with another man as with a woman, both men have committed a detestable act. They must both be put to death, for they are guilty of a capital offense.

1 John 1:9 (KJV)
If we confess our sins, he is faithful and just to forgive us our sins, and to cleanse us from all unrighteousness.

28. DOES GOD HATE HOMOSEXUALS SINCE HE CONDEMNED THEM TO DEATH IN THE OLD TESTAMENT OF THE BIBLE?

Not at all; not only does God have an unconditional love for homosexuals He loves all sinners (people). God hates sin, not sinners. Just because God or His Word does not agree with sin, this doesn't mean there is a lack of love present. His hatred of sin was greatly displayed when Jesus was being crucified on the cross; Jesus cried: "*My God, My God, why have You abandoned Me*". It was our sins on His Son that God refused to share. Even when Jesus needed God the most, our sins separated God to rescue even His sinless Son.

Some facts; it was not only homosexuality that God condemned to death a penalty. The following are a few additional sins that had death penalties as well:

- Murders (Genesis 9:6, Exodus 21:12 and Leviticus 24:17)
- Striking your parent (Exodus 21:15)
- Kidnappers (Exodus 21:16)
- Cursing your parents (Exodus 21:17 and Leviticus 20:9)
- Committing adultery (Leviticus 20:10-12)
- Committing fornication (Leviticus 20:13-14)
- Practicing bestiality Leviticus 20:15-16
- Mediums (psychic) or a wizards (magician or sorcerer) (Leviticus 20:27)
- If a priest daughter become a prostitute (Leviticus 21:9)
- Marriage violations for lying about virginity (Deuteronomy 22:20-21)

It is because of God's love, grace and mercy that most of these penalties have been lifted. However, lifting the severity does mean there are no consequences for the disobediences of them.

God is such a gentleman; He doesn't force His love on us and make us love Him in return. He gave His very best for all sinners, through **JESUS**!

Matthew 27:46 (AMP)
And about the ninth hour (three o'clock) Jesus cried with a loud voice, Eli, Eli, lama sabachthani?—that is, My God, My God, why have You abandoned Me [leaving Me helpless, forsaking and failing Me in My need]?

John 3:16-17 (AMP)
[16] For God so greatly loved and dearly prized the world that He [even] gave up His only begotten (unique) Son, so that whoever believes in (trusts in, clings to, relies on) Him shall not perish (come to destruction, be lost) but have eternal (everlasting) life.
[17] For God did not send the Son into the world in order to judge (to reject, to condemn, to pass sentence on) the world, but that the world might find salvation and be made safe and sound through Him.

Romans 5:8-10 (TLB)
[8] But God showed his great love for us by sending Christ to die for us while we were still sinners.
[9] And since by his blood he did all this for us as sinners, how much more will he do for us now that he has declared us not guilty? Now he will save us from all of God's wrath to come.
[10] And since, when we were his enemies, we were brought back to God by the death of his Son, what blessings he must have for us now that we are his friends and he is living within us!

Romans 8:38-39 (TLB)
³⁸ For I am convinced that nothing can ever separate us from his love. Death can't, and life can't. The angels won't, and all the powers of hell itself cannot keep God's love away. Our fears for today, our worries about tomorrow,
³⁹ or where we are—high above the sky, or in the deepest ocean—nothing will ever be able to separate us from the love of God demonstrated by our Lord Jesus Christ when he died for us.

2 Peter 3:9 (AMP)
The Lord does not delay and is not tardy or slow about what He promises, according to some people's conception of slowness, but He is long-suffering (extraordinarily patient) toward you, not desiring that any should perish, but that all should turn to repentance.

---

29. SINCE I WAS A LITTLE GIRL, I HAVE BEEN CURIOUS ABOUT MY SEXUALLY AND BEING WITH ANOTHER FEMALE, SINCE I'M A TEEN NOW. WHAT DO I DO WITH THESE FEELINGS?

Find help in a healthy and positive adult who will guide you to TRUTH through these feelings. This is so; you can make the right choice regarding your sexuality. It may not be that you want to be with a girl sexually, you may be going through your puberty stages and your body is developing in ways unfamiliar to you.

It also could be a lack/void in your life, seeking fulfillment. Maybe you need more attention from your mom or dad. It could be your best friends are getting more attention then you, so you're seeking another female's attention. Also, you may feel risky because you have heard, saw, smelled something or someone may have touched you in an unfamiliar way that could have unknowingly aroused your curiosity.

Once you open your spirit to same gender sexual behavior, it is not easy to turn back to the innocence within you. Any ungodly sexual encounters will hinder a period of time in experiencing God's best in your sexuality. God created sex as an enjoyable and pleasurable experience only to be enjoyed in Holy matrimony (marriage - the way He prepared it to be). Therefore, when any sexual act is done out of His guidelines, the ending results could be very damaging and unfulfilling.

> Romans 8:6 (KJV)
> For to be carnally minded *is* death; but to be spiritually minded *is* life and peace.
>
> 2 Corinthians 3:17 (KJV)
> Now the Lord is that Spirit: and where the Spirit of the Lord *is*, there *is* liberty.
>
> 2 Corinthians 10:3-4 (TLB)
> ³ It is true that I am an ordinary, weak human being, but I don't use human plans and methods to win my battles.
> ⁴ I use God's mighty weapons, not those made by men, to knock down the devil's strongholds.
>
> 2 Timothy 2:22 (KJV)
> Now flee from youthful lusts and pursue righteousness, faith, love and peace, with those who call on the Lord from a pure heart.

1 John 2:16 (KJV)
For all that is in the world, the lust of the flesh, and the lust of the eyes, and the pride of life, is not of the Father, but is of the world.

30. My grandmother agrees with my female partner and I being in a lesbian relationship. It must be okay, right?

Just because your grandmother agrees with your behavior in this lifestyle, does not make it right in the eyes of God. Unfortunately, your grandmother's love for you will not outweigh the consequences of this sin before God when you leave this earth, at the time of eternal judgment. Scriptures tells us that we cannot pay the penalty of someone else's sin; therefore when you stand before God your grandmother can not pay your sin debt, only Jesus can.

The beauty of this is you, your female partner, and your grandmother still have time to repent and come to God to receive salvation. This is God's desire for us all. Then, you can be sure your eternal destiny will be in heaven.

Proverbs 14:12 & 16:25 (KJV)
There is a way which seemeth right unto a man, but the end thereof are the ways of death.

Acts 17:30-31 (NLT)
[30] "God overlooked people's ignorance about these things in earlier times, but now he commands everyone everywhere to repent of their sins and turn to him.

³¹ For he has set a day for judging the world with justice by the man he has appointed, and he proved to everyone who this is by raising him from the dead."

Romans 1:26-27 & 32 (TLB)
²⁶ That is why God let go of them and let them do all these evil things, so that even their women turned against God's natural plan for them and indulged in sex sin with each other.
²⁷ And the men, instead of having normal sex relationships with women, burned with lust for each other, men doing shameful things with other men and, as a result, getting paid within their own souls with the penalty they so richly deserved.

³² They were fully aware of God's death penalty for these crimes, yet they went right ahead and did them anyway and encouraged others to do them, too.

Romans 5:19-21 (TLB)
¹⁹ Adam caused many to be sinners because he disobeyed God, and Christ caused many to be made acceptable to God because he obeyed.
²⁰ The Ten Commandments were given so that all could see the extent of their failure to obey God's laws. But the more we see our sinfulness, the more we see God's abounding grace forgiving us.
²¹ Before, sin ruled over all men and brought them to death, but now God's kindness rules instead, giving us right standing with God and resulting in eternal life through Jesus Christ our Lord.

Romans 14:11-12 (NIV)
¹¹ It is written: "'As surely as I live,' says the Lord, 'every knee will bow before me; every tongue will acknowledge God.'"
¹² So then, each of us will give an account of ourselves to God.

---

31. WHAT ABOUT PEOPLE NOW SAYING THAT GOD IS LOVE, SO WE SHOULD BE ABLE TO LOVE ONE ANOTHER IN HOMOSEXUAL RELATIONSHIPS? SINCE THE BIBLE TELLS US TO LOVE. FURTHERMORE, THERE ARE ONLY A FEW SCRIPTURES AGAINST HOMOSEXUALITY.

God truly is **Love** and with His loving-kindness He is strictly against homosexual relationships. This type of agreement would be against His divine holiness. If He wanted us to have this liberty, He would have given this teaching to us in the Bible. Since He first said: "No" to homosexuality; "No" means "No" throughout the bible to any homosexual relationships.

Any individual who takes the truth of God and make it a lie is in serious danger. Jesus clearly tells us *"if we love Him, then obey His commandments"* (the entire Bible). It is one thing to misunderstand scripture, but it is a serious matter when it is deliberately twisted for personal gain.

John 14:15 (AMP)
Jesus said: If you [really] love Me, you will keep (obey) My commands.

1 Timothy 1:9-11 (NLT)
⁹ For the law was not intended for people who do what is right. It is for people who are lawless and rebellious, who are ungodly and sinful, who consider nothing sacred and defile what is holy, who kill their father or mother or commit other murders.
¹⁰ The law is for people who are sexually immoral, or who practice homosexuality, or are slave traders, liars, promise breakers, or who do anything else that contradicts the wholesome teaching
¹¹ that comes from the glorious Good News entrusted to me by our blessed God.

1 Timothy 2:3-4 (KJV)
³ For this is good and acceptable in the sight of God our Saviour;
⁴ Who will have all men to be saved, and to come unto the knowledge of the truth.

1 John 4:5-10 (KJV)
⁵ They are of the world: therefore speak they of the world, and the world heareth them.
⁶ We are of God: he that knoweth God heareth us; he that is not of God heareth not us. Hereby know we the spirit of truth, and the spirit of error.
⁷ Beloved, let us love one another: for love is of God; and every one that loveth is born of God, and knoweth God.
⁸ He that loveth not knoweth not God; for God is love.
⁹ In this was manifested the love of God toward us, because that God sent his only begotten Son into the world, that we might live through him.

[10] Herein is love, not that we loved God, but that he loved us, and sent his Son to be the propitiation for our sins.

Revelation 22:18 & 19 (NLT)
[18] And I solemnly declare to everyone who hears the words of prophecy written in this book: If anyone adds anything to what is written here, God will add to that person the plagues described in this book.
[19] And if anyone removes any of the words from this book of prophecy, God will remove that person's share in the tree of life and in the holy city that are described in this book.

32. CAN A PERSON REALLY CHANGE FROM BEING HOMOSEXUAL ALL OF THEIR LIFE (OVER 20 YEARS) TO BECOME HETEROSEXUAL?

Our focus should be becoming as God has created us and not just about our sexuality. We were created to be much more than sexual human beings; this is the world's way of thinking. In 1 Corinthians 6:11, it reads: *"we once were like that."* So this is enough proof that anyone can change if he or she allows God to change them and set them free.

By now, I hope you had a chance to read my testimony to see how many times *"I tried."* But when I allowed God to be God, it was He who changed me. I couldn't do it in my own strength and I have not met anyone else who could fight this kind of stronghold sin in their strength. It is the power through Jesus' shed blood on Calvary's cross that will set you free!

John 6:37 (KJV)
All that the Father giveth me shall come to me; and him that cometh to me I will in no wise cast out.

Romans 8:13 (KJV)
For if ye live after the flesh, ye shall die: but if ye through the Spirit do mortify the deeds of the body, ye shall live.

1 Corinthians 6:9-11 (NLT)
[9] Don't you realize that those who do wrong will not inherit the Kingdom of God? Don't fool yourselves. Those who indulge in sexual sin, or who worship idols, or commit adultery, or are male prostitutes, or practice homosexuality,
[10] or are thieves, or greedy people, or drunkards, or are abusive, or cheat people—none of these will inherit the Kingdom of God.
[11] Some of you were once like that. But you were cleansed; you were made holy; you were made right with God by calling on the name of the Lord Jesus Christ and by the Spirit of our God.

Ephesians 2:1-5 (NLT)
[1] Once you were dead because of your disobedience and your many sins.
[2] You used to live in sin, just like the rest of the world, obeying the devil--the commander of the powers in the unseen world. He is the spirit at work in the hearts of those who refuse to obey God.
[3] All of us used to live that way, following the passionate desires and inclinations of our sinful nature. By our very nature we were subject to God's anger, just like everyone else.

⁴ But God is so rich in mercy, and he loved us so much,
⁵ that even though we were dead because of our sins, he gave us life when he raised Christ from the dead. (It is only by God's grace that you have been saved!)

Jude 1:24-25 (KJV)
²⁴ Now unto him that is able to keep you from falling, and to present you faultless before the presence of his glory with exceeding joy,
²⁵ To the only wise God our Saviour, be glory and majesty, dominion and power, both now and ever. Amen.

33. IS IT POSSIBLE TO LIVE IN A HOMOSEXUAL LIFESTYLE AND BE A FOLLOWER OF JESUS CHRIST?

The two key words here are "LIFESTYLE" and "FOLLOWER":

Lifestyle is our way of life, therefore if this way of life is contrary to the way Jesus asks us to live then it is against Him.

John 14:15 (AMP)
Jesus said: If you [really] love Me, you will keep (obey) My commands.

Follower is a supporter of someone, so in this case it is Jesus Christ. Again, if it is contrary to the way Jesus asks us to follow Him then it is against Him.

Matthew 12:30 (NLT)
Jesus said: "Anyone who isn't with me opposes me, and anyone who isn't working with me is actually working against me.

Luke 9:23 (KJV)
Jesus said: And he said to *them* all, If any *man* will come after me, let him deny himself, and take up his cross daily, and follow me.

God also said this because he desires you to choose <u>His way over your way</u>:

Revelation 3:15-16 (NIV)
15 I know your deeds, that you are neither cold nor hot. I wish you were either one or the other!
16 So, because you are lukewarm—neither hot nor cold—I am about to spit you out of my mouth.

Lastly, the Bible warns us that homosexuality is sin and against God's laws:

Leviticus 18:22 (NLT)
"Do not practice homosexuality, having sex with another man as with a woman. It is a detestable sin.

Leviticus 20:13 (NLT)
"If a man practices homosexuality, having sex with another man as with a woman, both men have committed a detestable act. They must both be put to death, for they are guilty of a capital offense.

34. Everyone I meet thinks I am a female since my reconstruction surgery, but I'm saved now. Should I change back to reflect the male gender as I was born?

For surgical reversal, seek counsel from your doctor and pastor about this decision if you truly desire change in this area. However, a currently resolution can be change in your dress attire. Some individuals wear looser clothing to conceal enhanced physiques.

There are many wonderful testimonies of other transgender persons Christian and non-Christian, which took a bold step of reinvesting to undo their surgical procedures. I believe some of these individuals may have made this decision to take a bold stand for righteousness and godliness. Let the Holy Spirit lead and guide you into all truth.

Matthew 16:24-26 (KJV)
[24] Then said Jesus unto his disciples, If any man will come after me, let him deny himself, and take up his cross, and follow me.
[25] For whosoever will save his life shall lose it: and whosoever will lose his life for my sake shall find it.
[26] For what is a man profited, if he shall gain the whole world, and lose his own soul? or what shall a man give in exchange for his soul?

Romans 12:1-2 (NLT)
[1] And so, dear brothers and sisters, I plead with you to give your bodies to God because of all he has done for you. Let them be a living and holy

sacrifice—the kind he will find acceptable. This is truly the way to worship him.
² Don't copy the behavior and customs of this world, but let God transform you into a new person by changing the way you think. Then you will learn to know God's will for you, which is good and pleasing and perfect.

Then, the Apostle Paul here is speaking about food sacrificed to idols, but we cannot let our lifestyle be a hindrance to others who may be observing our Christian walk.

1 Corinthians 8:9 (KJV)
But take heed lest by any means this liberty of yours become a stumblingblock to them that are weak.

2 Corinthians 6:3 (NLT)
We live in such a way that no one will stumble because of us, and no one will find fault with our ministry.

35. IS THERE ANY SAME-SEX RELATIONSHIPS RECORDED IN THE BIBLE?

There are no recorded God approved same-sex relationships in the Bible. However, Genesis chapters 18 and 19, then Jude records the event of Sodom and Gomorrah being destroyed for their sinful ways and lifestyles. One of which that the young and old men of the city of Sodom insisted to have sex with the two angles who visited Lot's home as guest. Then in 1 Kings it mentions male cult prostitutes; more than likely these were men were having sexual relations with other men.

> Genesis 19:4-5 (NIV)
> [4] Before they had gone to bed, all the men from every part of the city of Sodom—both young and old—surrounded the house.
> [5] They called to Lot, "Where are the men who came to you tonight? Bring them out to us so that we can have sex with them."

> 1 Kings 14:24 (AMP)
> There were also sodomites (male cult prostitutes) in the land. They did all the abominations of the nations whom the Lord cast out before the Israelites.

> Jude 1:7 (TLB)
> And don't forget the cities of Sodom and Gomorrah and their neighboring towns, all full of lust of every kind, including lust of men for other men. Those cities were destroyed by fire and continue to be a warning to us that there is a hell in which sinners are punished.

36. THE BIBLE MENTIONS VERY CLOSE RELATIONSHIPS WITH RUTH AND NAOMI, DAVID AND JONATHAN, THEN DANIEL AND ASHPENAZ. WERE THESE SAME-SEX RELATIONSHIPS?

These were not at all same-sex relationships. When these individuals spoke of their love, compassion and unity with one another, this was out of sincere love. This was not polluted or perverted love, which is exceptionally rampant in our society today.

God destroyed Sodom and Gomorrah and the surrounding towns in the book of Genesis around 2067 BC. Since the people feared God's wrath for their involvement in such an abominable (terrible, awful, horrible, offensive and detestable) sin as homosexuality, they were still talking about it by the time Jude wrote his letter around 68 AD. Back in those days, people had respect, honor, and reverence for God. During this time period, they know these acts would result in severe penalties which was death. However, God is so merciful of us; He lifted the ban of death for practicing homosexuals.

Sadly today, people have a tendency of ignoring God's righteous standards. Perhaps individuals who continues to practice sin, has hopes He will ignore judgment against them for un-repented sin. When God says, *He will do something*, please believe, He will do just what He said He will do. God will not lie.

Numbers 23:19 (KJV)
God is not a man, that he should lie; neither the son of man, that he should repent: hath he said, and shall he not do it? or hath he spoken, and shall he not make it good?

Jude 1:7 (TLB)
And don't forget the cities of Sodom and Gomorrah and their neighboring towns, all full of lust of every kind, including lust of men for other men. Those cities were destroyed by fire and continue to be a warning to us that there is a hell in which sinners are punished.

Ruth and Naomi's relationship:

Ruth's admiration for her mother-in-law was so respectful that she wanted to continue caring for her after Naomi's son passed away (Ruth's husband). She learned how to serve and fear God from Naomi. Therefore, the God fearing relationship she gains from this mentorship was so essential; she did not want to go back to her family's home and not continue to grow in her faith.

> Ruth 1:16-17 (KJV)
> [16] And Ruth said, Intreat me not to leave thee, or to return from following after thee: for whither thou goest, I will go; and where thou lodgest, I will lodge: thy people shall be my people, and thy God my God:
> [17] Where thou diest, will I die, and there will I be buried: the Lord do so to me, and more also, if ought but death part thee and me.

David and Johnathon's relationship:

There was an instant friendship bond between David and Jonathan; since David was graced with the favor of God on him. He comforted Jonathan's father, King Saul, when his mind was mentally disturbed. This demonstrated Jonathan's respect and love for David was genuine. Jonathan was very grateful to David since he helped his father out of distress.

> 1 Samuel 16:23 (KJV)
> And it came to pass, when the evil spirit from God was upon Saul, that David took an harp, and played with his hand: so Saul was refreshed, and was well, and the evil spirit departed from him.

1 Samuel 18:3 (KJV)
Then Jonathan and David made a covenant, because he loved him as his own soul.

Daniel and Ashpenaz:

This tender love mentioned here, is God's favor and grace to Daniel. This favor happened through Ashpenaz, the chief official for Jehoiakim who was king of Judah. He feared the king's anger if Daniel would appear unhealthy, since Ashpenaz was assigned to provide Daniel's food. More importantly, Ashpenaz feared for his own life.

We see this kind of kind-heartedness when individuals show favor for employment opportunities, business transactions and so forth.

Daniel 1:9 (KJV)
Now God had brought Daniel into favor and tender love with the prince of the eunuchs.

37. DID JESUS MENTION ANYTHING ABOUT SAME-SEX MARRIAGE OR HOMOSEXUALITY?

The scriptures that Jesus mentioned regarding marriage speak of a man and a woman. Man's laws are not God's laws and since we must give an account of our lives to God and Him alone; we should be most interested in what He hath said on this matter.

I believe Jesus specifically didn't mention anything regarding same-sex marriage or homosexuality because it was very clear of what happened in Noah's days, than to Sodom, Gomorrah, and the surrounding cities. Jesus mentioned in Luke 17:25-30, people went about their daily lives; *"They ate, they drank, they bought, they sold, they planted, they built and married";* which the same is going on today. (However, our society has added same-sex marriage to this list). Then Jesus said, *"He will be revealed".* The scriptures are very clear, any form of sexual sin including homosexuality was seriously forbidden by God and the consequences are very severe!

Jesus speaking in each of these passages of scripture:

Matthew 15:19-20 (NIV)
[19] For out of the heart come evil thoughts—murder, adultery, sexual immorality, theft, false testimony, slander.
[20] These are what defile a person; but eating with unwashed hands does not defile them."

Matthew 19:4-6 (AMP)
[4] He replied, Have you never read that He Who made them from the beginning made them male and female,
[5] And said, For this reason a man shall leave his father and mother and shall be united firmly (joined inseparably) to his wife, and the two shall become one flesh?
[6] So they are no longer two, but one flesh. What therefore God has joined together, let not man put asunder (separate).

Mark 10:5-9 (AMP)
⁵ But Jesus said to them, Because of your hardness of heart your condition of insensibility to the call of God] he wrote you this precept in your Law.
⁶ But from the beginning of creation God made them male and female.
⁷ For this reason a man shall leave [behind] his father and his mother and be joined to his wife and cleave closely to her permanently,
⁸ And the two shall become one flesh, so that they are no longer two, but one flesh.
⁹ What therefore God has united (joined together), let not man separate *or* divide.

Luke 17:25-30 (ASV)
²⁵ But first must he suffer many things and be rejected of this generation.
²⁶ And as it came to pass in the days of Noah, even so shall it be also in the days of the Son of man.
²⁷ They ate, they drank, they married, they were given in marriage, until the day that Noah entered into the ark, and the flood came, and destroyed them all.
²⁸ Likewise even as it came to pass in the days of Lot; they ate, they drank, they bought, they sold, they planted, they builded;
²⁹ but in the day that Lot went out from Sodom it rained fire and brimstone from heaven, and destroyed them all:
³⁰ after the same manner shall it be in the day that the Son of man is revealed.

> **38. IT SEEMS THAT THE NUMBER OF PEOPLE WHO ARE PROMOTING SAME-SEX MARRIAGE AND HOMOSEXUAL LIFESTYLES IS ON THE RISE. WHAT ARE YOUR THOUGHTS ABOUT THIS?**

I can say plenty, but at this point my thoughts are to obey and agree with God and Him alone. Our lives start with God and will end with God's acceptance of judgment. It is He that will have the final word. We are solely accountable to Him with what we believe and the actions done with our lives. The final authority is His laws of righteousness through the Holy Bible.

<u>Let's explore what God says in His Word</u>:

Proverbs 1:24-32 (NLV)
[24] I called but you would not listen. I put out my hand and no one gave it a thought.
[25] You did not listen when I told you what you should do, and you would not hear any of my strong words.
[26] So I will laugh at your trouble. I will laugh when you are afraid.
[27] Fear will come to you like a storm. Hard times will come like a strong wind. When trouble and suffering come upon you,
[28] then they will call on me, but I will not answer. They will look for me, but they will not find me.
[29] Because they hated much learning, and did not choose the fear of the Lord.
[30] They would not listen when I told them what they should do. They laughed at all my strong words.
[31] So they will eat the fruit of their own way, and be filled with their own plans.

³² For the foolish will be killed by their turning away. The trust that fools put in themselves will destroy them.

Isaiah 3:11 (NIV)
Woe to the wicked! Disaster is upon them! They will be paid back for what their hands have done.

Isaiah 5:20 (NLT)
What sorrow for those who say that evil is good and good is evil, that dark is light and light is dark, that bitter is sweet and sweet is bitter.

Isaiah 48:22 (KJV)
There is no peace, saith the LORD, unto the wicked.

Romans 2:4-9 (NIV)
⁴ Or do you show contempt for the riches of his kindness, forbearance and patience, not realizing that God's kindness is intended to lead you to repentance?
⁵ But because of your stubbornness and your unrepentant heart, you are storing up wrath against yourself for the day of God's wrath, when his righteous judgment will be revealed.
⁶ God "will repay each person according to what they have done."
⁷ To those who by persistence in doing good seek glory, honor and immortality, he will give eternal life.
⁸ But for those who are self-seeking and who reject the truth and follow evil, there will be wrath and anger.

⁹ There will be trouble and distress for every human being who does evil: first for the Jew, then for the Gentile;

Romans 14:12 (KJV)
So then every one of us shall give account of himself to God.

2 Corinthians 5:10 (KJV)
For we must all appear before the judgment seat of Christ; that every one may receive the things done in his body, according to that he hath done, whether it be good or bad.

Galatians 6:7-8 (KJV)
⁷ Be not deceived; God is not mocked: for whatsoever a man soweth, that shall he also reap.
⁸ For he that soweth to his flesh shall of the flesh reap corruption; but he that soweth to the Spirit shall of the Spirit reap life everlasting.

39. WHY DOES IT SEEM THAT A NUMBER OF CHRISTIANS ARE SILENT OR NOW BELIEVING THE SAME-SEX MARRIAGE AGENDA?

The Bible has warned us of events prior to the end times of Jesus' return. These are signs that it is rapidly approaching! Scriptures have informed us that there will be a great falling away from the faith. Also, individuals have found teachers to teach these false teachings.

On the other hand, there are people that feel if they are not experienced or an expert in a subject then it is best not to say anything. It also could be out of fear of rejection and persecution, since it seems the majority on this subject is ruling.

I am a firm believer in the Holy Spirit that He will lead us into all truths as well as, continually seeking God's Word for truth. The beauty is in God's supreme wisdom. He is elevating many individuals, as well as me, to be His mouth piece to speak truth.

Even though I lived many years struggling in and living out a lesbian lifestyle, I cannot claim to know everything on this subject. And, maybe not enough to even debate someone on this subject. Critics may win an argument, but ultimately God's Word will prevail.

For an example, in the days of Abraham and Lot, the majority of people in Sodom and Gomorrah were in agreement with sexual sins; however they collectively lost their lives as a result of their decisions (Genesis 19:1-29).

Ephesians 5:6 (ASV)
Let no man deceive you with empty words: for because of these things cometh the wrath of God upon the sons of disobedience.

2 Thessalonians 2:3-4 (AMP)
³ Let no one deceive *or* beguile you in any way, for that day will not come except the apostasy comes first [unless the predicted great falling away of those who have professed to be Christians has come], and the man of lawlessness (sin) is revealed, who is the son of doom (of perdition),
⁴ Who opposes and exalts himself so proudly *and* insolently against *and* over all that is called God

or that is worshiped, [even to his actually] taking his seat in the temple of God, proclaiming that he himself is God.

2 Timothy 3:13 (TLB)
In fact, evil men and false teachers will become worse and worse, deceiving many, they themselves having been deceived by Satan.

2 Timothy 4:3-4 (TLB)
³ For there is going to come a time when people won't listen to the truth but will go around looking for teachers who will tell them just what they want to hear.
⁴ They won't listen to what the Bible says but will blithely follow their own misguided ideas.

<u>These passages of scriptures are to encourage individuals to trust God for strength:</u>

1 Chronicles 16:21-22 (KJV)
²¹ He suffered no man to do them wrong: yea, he reproved kings for their sakes,
²² *Saying*, Touch not mine anointed, and do my prophets no harm.

Isaiah 54:17 (NLT)
But in that coming day no weapon turned against you will succeed. You will silence every voice raised up to accuse you. These benefits are enjoyed by the servants of the LORD; their vindication will come from me. I, the LORD, have spoken!

Galatians 1:10 (KJV)
For do I now persuade men, or God? or do I seek to please men? for if I yet pleased men, I should not be the servant of Christ.

2 Peter 2:6-9 (NLT)
⁶ Later, God condemned the cities of Sodom and Gomorrah and turned them into heaps of ashes. He made them an example of what will happen to ungodly people.
⁷ But God also rescued Lot out of Sodom because he was a righteous man who was sick of the shameful immorality of the wicked people around him.
⁸ Yes, Lot was a righteous man who was tormented in his soul by the wickedness he saw and heard day after day.
⁹ So you see, the Lord knows how to rescue godly people from their trials, even while keeping the wicked under punishment until the day of final judgment.

STD'S IN OUR COMMUNITIES - SEXUALLY TRANSMITTED DEMONIC SPIRITS

This chapter is very important. It will expose how spirits enter into humans and infect their lives. We must remember that we are natural and spiritual beings. We have a soul and spirit that is housed inside our bodies. It is the spirit and soul that is influenced by either God's Holy Spirit or contaminated evil spirits. If evil spirits are not properly evicted, they will remain or multiply. Ultimately, the body will follow the spirit that has the most control.

> 1 Thessalonians 5:23 (KJV)
> And the very God of peace sanctify you wholly; and I pray God your whole spirit and soul and body be preserved blameless unto the coming of our Lord Jesus Christ.

> Luke 11:26 also Matthew 12:45 (KJV)
> Then goeth he, and taketh to him seven other spirits more wicked than himself; and they enter in, and dwell there: and the last state of that man is worse than the first.

40. WHAT ARE SOUL TIES?

The basis of a soul tie happens when an individual has physical and/or emotional connections with another person beyond the norm. Their soul becomes entangled with the other person. This can happen emotionally; without having sexual relations or physically; past a one night stand or a long term relationship. However, there are different kinds of soul ties, good and bad ones.

When a person has a bad soul tie, they are usually in denial or not willing to face the pain of it. Bad soul ties will leave unseen emotional and mental scars; as well as wounds long beyond the dissolution of the relationship.

Think of two glued pieces of cardboard, they do not pull apart evenly or clean. Each side is left with residue from the other side. This is the result of how a bad soul tie can leave damaging pieces to another person's heart and soul. It could take months, years, even decades to pull away all of the fragmented pieces.

Let's review bad soul ties first, according to the Bible:

> Genesis 34:1-4 (NIV)
> [1] Now Dinah, the daughter Leah had borne to Jacob, went out to visit the women of the land.
> [2] When Shechem son of Hamor the Hivite, the ruler of that area, saw her, he took her and raped her.
> [3] His heart was drawn to Dinah daughter of Jacob; he loved the young woman and spoke tenderly to her.

⁴ And Shechem said to his father Hamor, "Get me this girl as my wife."

2 Samuel 13:1-2 (NLT)
¹ Now David's son Absalom had a beautiful sister named Tamar. And Amnon, her half brother, fell desperately in love with her.
² Amnon became so obsessed with Tamar that he became ill. She was a virgin, and Amnon thought he could never have her.

Ezekiel 23:17 (AMP)
And the Babylonians came to her into the bed of love, and they defiled her with their evil desire; and when she was polluted by them, she [Jerusalem] broke the relationship *and* pushed them away from her in disgust.

1 Corinthians 6:16 (KJV)
What? know ye not that he which is joined to an harlot is one body? for two, saith he, shall be one flesh.

Then Bible also describes good soul ties, which are God ordained:

There was an instant friendship bond between David and Jonathan; since David was graced with the favor of God on him. He comforted Jonathan's father, King Saul, when his mind was mentally disturbed. This demonstrated Jonathan's respect and love for David was genuine. Jonathan was grateful to David since he helped his father out of distress.

1 Samuel 16:23 (KJV)
And it came to pass, when the evil spirit from God was upon Saul, that David took an harp, and

played with his hand: so Saul was refreshed, and was well, and the evil spirit departed from him.

1 Samuel 18:1 (KJV)
And it came to pass, when he had made an end of speaking unto Saul, that the soul of Jonathan was knit with the soul of David, and Jonathan loved him as his own soul.

According to Acts 4:32-37; the people were of one heart and one soul as believers in Jesus Christ. They shared everything they owned with one another and no one was left in poverty. God's grace was so mightily at work within them.

Acts 4:32 (KJV)
And the multitude of them that believed were of one heart and of one soul: neither said any of them that ought of the things which he possessed was his own; but they had all things common.

Another God ordained soul tie; happens when He rewards a man and a woman marriage in Holy Matrimony:

Genesis 2:24, Matthew 19:5, Mark 10:7 and Ephesians 5:31 (KJV)
Therefore shall a man leave his father and his mother, and shall cleave unto his wife: and they shall be one flesh.

Proverbs 18:22 (NLT)
The man who finds a wife finds a treasure, and he receives favor from the Lord

Matthew 19:6 (KJV)
Wherefore they are no more twain, but one flesh. What therefore God hath joined together, let not man put asunder.

41. HOW DO I HELP MY CHILD SEVER A SOUL TIE?

You are on the right track as a parent to seek help for your child, since soul ties are dangerous and damaging. Loved ones are usually the persons to notice it, with desires for this individual to receive freedom, healing and wholeness. Most often, this person is usually in denial that his (her) desires or past relationship has a corrupt grip on them. Intercession is in order to break this bondage.

I remember as a youth, I had a really good friend and we made an oath with one another. We pricked our finger and exchanged blood to represent our bond as best friends or "*blood sisters*", which symbolized our closeness as friends. However, we lost contact after becoming adults and our lives took different paths. When I accepted Jesus as my Lord and Savior, I renounced in prayer that agreement and severed that soul tie. This may sound minor to some, but we must be careful of oaths made as youth and adults (read Philippians 4:6). According to, Proverbs 18:21, *"there is power in what we speak".*

Therefore, when your loved one is ready for help; lead them through prayers of forgiveness (for sins and any un-forgiveness's), confessions (to denounce all connections in the past, present or future) and restoration (faith that they have received freedom through Christ Jesus). If you feel you are not the person to facilitate this deliverance, please find a spiritual leader to assist to break this oppression.

Proverbs 18:21 (AMP)
Death and life are in the power of the tongue, and they who indulge in it shall eat the fruit of it [for death or life].

Colossians 1:9 (ASV)
For this cause we also, since the day we heard it, do not cease to pray and make request for you, that ye may be filled with the knowledge of his will in all spiritual wisdom and understanding,

1 Timothy 2:1-4 (KJV)
[1] I exhort therefore, that, first of all, supplications, prayers, intercessions, and giving of thanks, be made for all men;
[2] For kings, and for all that are in authority; that we may lead a quiet and peaceable life in all godliness and honesty.
[3] For this is good and acceptable in the sight of God our Saviour;
[4] Who will have all men to be saved, and to come unto the knowledge of the truth.

The Bible promises freedom from bad soul ties if we obey God's laws. Freedom is a choice.

Romans 10:9-10 (KJV)
[9] That if thou shalt confess with thy mouth the Lord Jesus, and shalt believe in thine heart that God hath raised him from the dead, thou shalt be saved.

¹⁰ For with the heart man believeth unto righteousness; and with the mouth confession is made unto salvation.

1 Corinthians 6:17-18 (AMP)
¹⁷ But the person who is united to the Lord becomes one spirit with Him.
¹⁸ Shun immorality *and* all sexual looseness [flee from impurity in thought, word, or deed]. Any other sin which a man commits is one outside the body, but he who commits sexual immorality sins against his own body.

Galatians 5:1 (KJV)
Stand fast therefore in the liberty wherewith Christ hath made us free, and be not entangled again with the yoke of bondage.

Ephesians 3:20-21 (KJV)
²⁰ Now unto him that is able to do exceeding abundantly above all that we ask or think, according to the power that worketh in us,
²¹ Unto him be glory in the church by Christ Jesus throughout all ages, world without end. Amen.

42. How can a Homosexual Spirit Gain Access into a Human?

- Generational Sins (also known as curses)
- Control, Influence and Seduction
- Transferring of Spirits
- Experimentation
- Rejection
- Pride

Please note; this particular information will discuss demonic spirits entry ways for homosexuality. However, all ungodly sexual perversions provide access to demonic spirits; since these relations are out of the will of God.

1st – Spirits can gain access by attaching themselves spiritually to the child in the mother's womb, which could be the results from sins of a parent or a family generation. This entree is known as generational sins which gives demonic spirits access. This is the reason why some individuals have shared that they have felt same-sex attractions as an adolescent. However, everyone who experiences homosexuality isn't going through a generational sin. Some individuals have no trace of this lifestyle in their family genes.

There are people that believe generational sins are extinct. However, this has been proven incorrect time after time in countless incidents. I have witnessed in my personal linage, including my current family bloodline, there were and currently are several practicing homosexuals. This would be a sure coincidence if this was a lifestyle we all happen to battle. Besides, after serving in jails and prisons for many years now, I have met countless individuals whose parents and other family members has committed exact crimes for decades. Therefore, these example prove generational sins still exists.

On the other hand, if an individual is confessing Christianity and living in ways that are disobedient to God's Word; they are opening doors to demonic forces to regain access. Jesus warns us, when this happens these demonic forces come back seven times worst.

> Exodus 20:4-6 (AMP)
> [4] You shall not make yourself any graven image [to worship it] or any likeness of anything that is in the heavens above, or that is in the earth beneath, or that is in the water under the earth;
> [5] You shall not bow down yourself to them or serve them; for I the Lord your God am a jealous God, visiting the iniquity of the fathers upon the children to the third and fourth generation of those who hate Me,
> [6] But showing mercy *and* steadfast love to a thousand generations of those who love Me and keep My commandments.

> Deuteronomy 30:19 (AMP)
> I call heaven and earth to witness this day against you that I have set before you life and death, the blessings and the curses; therefore choose life, that you and your descendants may live.

> Hosea 4:6 (KJV)
> My people are destroyed for lack of knowledge: because thou hast rejected knowledge, I will also reject thee, that thou shalt be no priest to me:

seeing thou hast forgotten the law of thy God, I will also forget thy children.

Matthew 12:45 also Luke 11:26 (KJV)
Then goeth he, and taketh with himself seven other spirits more wicked than himself, and they enter in and dwell there: and the last state of that man is worse than the first. Even so shall it be also unto this wicked generation.

Evil spirits are always present to tempt, entice and lure individuals into any kind of sin. However, we have the power of choice to choose, which gives us resilience to temptations. This repellency is done through the power of Jesus Christ. Generational sin through a family bloodline (natural) is broken through Christ blood (spiritual). He became a curse for us, so we can be redeemed from the curse of sin. Since we were naturally born into sin, Jesus explained; "**We must be born again**."

The key here is: we no longer must bear (carry) our parent's curse; however we have inherited (received) sin. God so graciously cleared us of the punishment of generational curses in the book of Ezekiel 18.

John 3:3 (KJV)
Jesus answered and said unto him, Verily, verily, I say unto thee, Except a man be born again, he cannot see the kingdom of God.

Ezekiel 18:14-22 (AMP)
[14] But if this wicked man begets a son who sees all the sins which his father has committed, and considers and fears [God] and does not do like his father,

¹⁵ Who has not eaten [food set before idols] upon the mountains nor has lifted up his eyes to the idols of the house of Israel, has not defiled his neighbor's wife,
¹⁶ Nor wronged anyone, nor has taken anything in pledge, nor has taken by robbery but has given his bread to the hungry and has covered the naked with a garment,
¹⁷ Who has withdrawn his hand from [oppressing] the poor, who has not received interest or increase [from the needy] but has executed My ordinances and has walked in My statutes; he shall not die for the iniquity of his father; he shall surely live.
¹⁸ As for his father, because he cruelly oppressed, robbed his brother, and did that which is not good among his people, behold, he shall die for his iniquity and guilt.
¹⁹ Yet do you say, Why does not the son bear the iniquity of the father? When the son has done that which is lawful and right and has kept all My statutes and has done them, he shall surely live.
²⁰ The soul that sins, it [is the one that] shall die. The son shall not bear and be punished for the iniquity of the father, neither shall the father bear and be punished for the iniquity of the son; the righteousness of the righteous shall be upon him only, and the wickedness of the wicked shall be upon the wicked only.
²¹ But if the wicked man turns from all his sins that he has committed and keeps all My statutes and does that which is lawful and right, he shall surely live; he shall not die.
²² None of his transgressions which he has committed shall be remembered against him; for his righteousness which he has executed [for his

moral and spiritual rectitude in every area and relation], he shall live.

Galatians 3:13-14 (KJV)
[13] Christ hath redeemed us from the curse of the law, being made a curse for us: for it is written, Cursed is every one that hangeth on a tree:
[14] That the blessing of Abraham might come on the Gentiles through Jesus Christ; that we might receive the promise of the Spirit through faith.

God is longsuffering and He continuously extends His mercy to us. He gives us power to break generational sins with His generational blessings, when we obey Him.

Job 8:4-6 (NLT)
[4] Your children must have sinned against him, so their punishment was well deserved.
[5] But if you pray to God and seek the favor of the Almighty,
[6] and if you are pure and live with integrity, he will surely rise up and restore your happy home.

Psalm 103:17-18 (TLB)
[17-18] But the loving-kindness of the Lord is from everlasting to everlasting to those who reverence him; his salvation is to children's children of those who are faithful to his covenant and remember to obey him!

Romans 5:17 (KJV)
For if by one man's offence death reigned by one; much more they which receive abundance of grace and of the gift of righteousness shall reign in life by one, Jesus Christ.

2ⁿᵈ – Spirits may gain access through a spirit of control, influence and seduction. When two individuals are sexually active their spirits become one. As well as, when a person yields their will to an abuser this may allow spirits to gain access.

> Proverbs 25:28 (KJV)
> He that hath no rule over his own spirit is like a city that is broken down, and without walls.

> 1 Corinthians 6:16-18 (AMP)
> ¹⁶ Or do you not know and realize that when a man joins himself to a prostitute, he becomes one body with her? The two, it is written, shall become one flesh.
> ¹⁷ But the person who is united to the Lord becomes one spirit with Him.
> ¹⁸ Shun immorality and all sexual looseness [flee from impurity in thought, word, or deed]. Any other sin which a man commits is one outside the body, but he who commits sexual immorality sins against his own body.

3ʳᵈ – Spirits can gain access during homosexual violence such as molestation or rape, this is also known as *"transferring of spirits"*. Since we are spiritual beings; 1 Corinthians 6:16-17 spoke about individuals being joined as *"one flesh"*. This gives spirits access through the trauma from experiencing fear, being bullied, deception, and even self-hatred. Because this sexual act wasn't exercised in love, the *"fear of it brings torment"* (evil spirits) according to 1 John 4:18.

John 10:10 (KJV)
The thief cometh not, but for to steal, and to kill, and to destroy: I am come that they might have life, and that they might have it more abundantly.

1 John 4:18 (KJV)
There is no fear in love; but perfect love casteth out fear: because fear hath torment. He that feareth is not made perfect in love.

4th – Spirits can gain access during sexual curiosity, which leads to experimentation. These occurrences can take place at youth gatherings such as sleepovers (as adolescents call it "*playing house*") and other youth gathering (peer pressure of "*I dare you*" games). Some adults also fall into this curiosity pressure after viewing pornography on the internet, in magazines, in some TV shows that bait them into same-sex attractions, as well as some music lyrics. This inquisitiveness or these imaginations lure individual's right into same-sex attractions and then relations.

Romans 7:15-20 (NIV)
^{15} I do not understand what I do. For what I want to do I do not do, but what I hate I do.
^{16} And if I do what I do not want to do, I agree that the law is good.
^{17} As it is, it is no longer I myself who do it, but it is sin living in me.
18 For I know that good itself does not dwell in me, that is, in my sinful nature. For I have the desire to do what is good, but I cannot carry it out.
^{19} For I do not do the good I want to do, but the evil I do not want to do—this I keep on doing.

²⁰ Now if I do what I do not want to do, it is no longer I who do it, but it is sin living in me that does it.

5ᵗʰ – Spirits can gain access through rejection (disobedience against God's will). This rejection can originate from hurts of relationships with the opposite sex, need of human approval, lack of love, etc., which can lead to multiple sexual partners for fulfillment. Unfortunately, these individuals <u>reject trusting God</u> to heal their hurt and pain, therefore this allow spirits to have free reign.

Matthew 12:43-45 also Luke 11:24-26 (KJV)
Jesus said: ⁴³ When the unclean spirit is gone out of a man, he walketh through dry places, seeking rest, and findeth none.
⁴⁴ Then he saith, I will return into my house from whence I came out; and when he is come, he findeth it empty, swept, and garnished.
⁴⁵ Then goeth he, and taketh with himself seven other spirits more wicked than himself, and they enter in and dwell there: and the last state of that man is worse than the first. Even so shall it be also unto this wicked generation.

Romans 1:24-32 (TLB)
²⁴ So God let them go ahead into every sort of sex sin, and do whatever they wanted to—yes, vile and sinful things with each other's bodies.
²⁵ Instead of believing what they knew was the truth about God, they deliberately chose to believe lies. So they prayed to the things God made, but wouldn't obey the blessed God who made these things.

²⁶ That is why God let go of them and let them do all these evil things, so that even their women turned against God's natural plan for them and indulged in sex sin with each other.

²⁷ And the men, instead of having normal sex relationships with women, burned with lust for each other, men doing shameful things with other men and, as a result, getting paid within their own souls with the penalty they so richly deserved.

²⁸ So it was that when they gave God up and would not even acknowledge him, God gave them up to doing everything their evil minds could think of.

²⁹ Their lives became full of every kind of wickedness and sin, of greed and hate, envy, murder, fighting, lying, bitterness, and gossip.

³⁰ They were backbiters, haters of God, insolent, proud, braggarts, always thinking of new ways of sinning and continually being disobedient to their parents.

³¹ They tried to misunderstand, broke their promises, and were heartless—without pity.

³² They were fully aware of God's death penalty for these crimes, yet they went right ahead and did them anyway and encouraged others to do them, too.

6th – The spirit of pride brings: narcissism, arrogance, excessive attention, rebelliousness, selfishness, overindulgence, etc. Therefore, allowing demonic spirits to gain access.

1 Samuel 15:23 (NLT)
Rebellion is as sinful as witchcraft, and stubbornness as bad as worshiping idols. So

because you have rejected the command of the LORD, he has rejected you as king." (*This message was to King Saul; however it applies to each of us as well when we reject God instructions*).

Proverbs 16:18-20 (KJV)
[18] Pride goeth before destruction, and an haughty spirit before a fall.
[19] Better it is to be of an humble spirit with the lowly, than to divide the spoil with the proud.
[20] He that handleth a matter wisely shall find good: and whoso trusteth in the LORD, happy is he.

Romans 1:22 (KJV)
Professing themselves to be wise, they became fools,

43. OCCASIONALLY I HAVE "WET DREAMS". WHY DO I HAVE ORGASMS WHILE I AM ASLEEP?

Please seek professional medical attention immediately, to ensure you are not experiencing internal chemical imbalances.

On a spiritual side, you may be experiencing sexual violations by incubus or succubus demonic spirits. This type of rape (*forced sexual intercourse upon a person without their consent or against their will*) is known to happen while a person is asleep. According to most dictionaries, you would find these demonic spirits mission is to bring on sexual oppressions and nightmares.

An incubus demonic spirit appears in the form of a male which usually rapes female. A succubus demonic spirit appears in the form of a female that usually rape men.

Other individuals have reported that they have experienced demonic spirits of the same gender forced intercourse. This happens when an incubus male demon rapes a male and the succubus female demon rapes a female. Their objective is to seduce the individual into a lifestyle of homosexuality.

There are consequences for every sin we commit. When we are involved in sexual sins, we sin against our own bodies (1 Corinthians 6:18). These consequences could lure demonic forces to attack our physical beings, bringing oppressions and nightmares.

I too experienced this torment by demonic spirits for many years, due to my promiscuous and lesbian lifestyle. When it first happened, I did not understand what was happening to my body. These demon spirits have a way to make their violation feel pleasurable with orgasms; but after a while they will torment the individual which is the ultimate mission of demons.

As I sought homosexual healing, I attended a Sexual and Relational Healing Retreat in Chicago, IL, where I learned about incubus and succubus demonic spirits. Shortly thereafter, I began spiritual counseling for deliverance. This led me to increase my time in prayer, fasting and reading God's Word. There were many days when I wanted to relax at home to watch a movie, go shopping with friends or attend family events; but the Lord required me to turn the television off and stay at home to fast and pray. I had to be very conscience of what I allowed into my spiritual being. That meant, I had to be very careful of what I watched on TV (no sex scenes), music lyrics (only Christian music), and deny myself (days of fasting for spiritual strength – when I decreased, Christ increased in me) St. John 3:30. This is how I overcame and continue to overcome these demonic attacks.

> Ephesians 6:10-17 (TLB)
> [10] Last of all I want to remind you that your strength must come from the Lord's mighty power within you.
> [11] Put on all of God's armor so that you will be able to stand safe against all strategies and tricks of Satan.
> [12] For we are not fighting against people made of flesh and blood, but against persons without bodies—the evil rulers of the unseen world, those mighty satanic beings and great evil princes of darkness who rule this world; and against huge numbers of wicked spirits in the spirit world.
> [13] So use every piece of God's armor to resist the enemy whenever he attacks, and when it is all over, you will still be standing up.
> [14] But to do this, you will need the strong belt of truth and the breastplate of God's approval.
> [15] Wear shoes that are able to speed you on as you preach the Good News of peace with God.
> [16] In every battle you will need faith as your shield to stop the fiery arrows aimed at you by Satan.
> [17] And you will need the helmet of salvation and the sword of the Spirit—which is the Word of God.

> James 4:7 (KJV)
> Submit yourselves therefore to God. Resist the devil, and he will flee from you.

Intimacy –

When the Enemy is "My Inner Me"

What do you think when you hear the word: e*nemy*? Do you think it is someone that is friendly toward you or someone who is against you? When selfness is your enemy, you are hindering your healing process. Jesus asked the paralyze man; *"Do you want to be made whole"* (St. John 5:6). The man began stating reasons why he could not be healed. Once you deny the enemy within and its selfish ways; healing will come.

---

44. IF AN INDIVIDUAL DESIRES TO COME OUT OF AN ADDICTION, IS IT DIFFICULT FOR HIM/HER TO TRULY BE FREE?

Having a desire is the first step, and then surrendering your life to God is imperative. Too often, individuals rely on society for remedies and they receive temporary help. This only serves as a bandage (covering). When an infected sore is covered, over time the wound under the covering doesn't receive the necessary cleaning treatment.

When this happens, the untreated sore can become a more serious problem.

We are spiritual beings and addictions happen in the spiritual realm; however it manifest in the natural realm. Commitment to God's plan of salvation and believing (having faith) that He will do it, is vital. These are crucial steps to the strength needed to come out of addictions and be free. (Please read section number 10 in this book for steps to salvation).

There are some wonderful Christian support groups to join in most communities. I recommend you find one. This will be very beneficial to your spiritual growth and help with accountability. Most habits are extremely difficult to break; but nothing is impossible or too hard for God.

> Jeremiah 32:17 (NIV)
> "Ah, Sovereign LORD, you have made the heavens and the earth by your great power and outstretched arm. Nothing is too hard for you.
>
> Matthew 17:20 (KJV)
> And Jesus said unto them, Because of your unbelief: for verily I say unto you, If ye have faith as a grain of mustard seed, ye shall say unto this mountain, Remove hence to yonder place; and it shall remove; and nothing shall be impossible unto you.
>
> Luke 18:27 (KJV)
> **_Jesus again speaking:_** And he said, The things which are impossible with men are possible with God.

1 Peter 5:7-8 (NIV)
⁷ Cast all your anxiety on him because he cares for you.
⁸ Be alert and of sober mind. Your enemy the devil prowls around like a roaring lion looking for someone to devour.

45. HOW DO I OVERCOME THE DIRTY FEELINGS IN MY HEART AND SOUL FROM MY PAST?

Take those dirty feelings which could be hatred, hurt, pain, shame, or even no self-worth to the Lord and leave them there. Let Him cleanse, strengthen and renew the broken spirit within you.

Even King David (which was a man after God's own heart) felt the same way after his sin was exposed by the Prophet Nathan. David became godly sorrowful, repented and prayed to God; *create in him a clean heart and renew a right spirit within him*. After receiving Christ as your Savior and the gift of the Holy Spirit, you will receive power to pray this prayer from the Bible to receive your cleansing and healing as well.

Psalm 51:10-12 (KJV)
¹⁰ Create in me a clean heart, O God; and renew a right spirit within me.
¹¹ Cast me not away from thy presence; and take not thy holy spirit from me.
¹² Restore unto me the joy of thy salvation; and uphold me with thy free spirit.

Psalm 103:10-12 (ASV)
¹⁰ He hath not dealt with us after our sins, Nor rewarded us after our iniquities.
¹¹ For as the heavens are high above the earth, So great is his lovingkindness toward them that fear him.
¹² As far as the east is from the west, So far hath he removed our transgressions from us.

Romans 10:11 (ASV)
For the scripture saith, Whosoever believeth on him shall not be put to shame.

Galatians 5:1 (KJV)
Stand fast therefore in the liberty wherewith Christ hath made us free, and be not entangled again with the yoke of bondage.

46. (FROM A MALE) SINCE I ACCEPTED JESUS AS MY SAVIOR, I STILL HAVE FEMININE CHARACTERISTICS. PEOPLE TEASE ME ABOUT THIS, WHAT SHOULD I DO?

This is so unfortunate and unkind. Know that, God is sitting high and looking low. There is no deed done that He will not judge. People criticized and even teased Jesus Christ who is perfect.

Time after time, individuals have made countless mistakes about a person's character and missed the wonderful person inside. Unfortunately, this has caused great pain in so many ways. If you know your heart is true with God, then go with that choice to follow Him.

It is important to find who you are and God's purpose for you. Your creator created you for a special reason and only He genuinely knows you.

Intimacy

Find your identity in Him and Him alone. When individuals are unaware of their value, they seek value in others. This is very dangerous and will not bring peace or happiness.

People are very inconsistent; one day they will love you and the next day they may hate you. If you solely base your life on what individuals say about you or what they think; then you will be a miserable person. Trust me; this is not the will of God for you.

Accountability is important as well. Find some godly men who are strong in their faith with God and ask them to mentor you. **Caution**, do not solely depend on these individuals to validate you. This may lead to codependency and that's a huge problem in itself, which you do not want to engage. Keep your heart clean. Turn everything within you over to God and watch Him transform and renew you!

God told this to Abraham, so now that you have accepted Jesus, you are a child of God to receive this promise as well:

Genesis 12:3 (NIV)
I will bless those who bless you, and whoever curses you I will curse; and all peoples on earth will be blessed through you."

1 Samuel 16:7 (KJV)
But the LORD said unto Samuel, Look not on his countenance, or on the height of his stature; because I have refused him: for *the LORD seeth* not as man seeth; for man looketh on the outward appearance, but the LORD looketh on the heart.

1 Peter 4:12-14 (NIV)
[12] Dear friends, do not be surprised at the fiery ordeal that has come on you to test you, as

though something strange were happening to you.
¹³ But rejoice inasmuch as you participate in the sufferings of Christ, so that you may be overjoyed when his glory is revealed.
¹⁴ If you are insulted because of the name of Christ, you are blessed, for the Spirit of glory and of God rests on you.

1 Peter 5:7-10 (KJV)
⁷ Casting all your care upon him; for he careth for you.
⁸ Be sober, be vigilant; because your adversary the devil, as a roaring lion, walketh about, seeking whom he may devour:
⁹ Whom resist stedfast in the faith, knowing that the same afflictions are accomplished in your brethren that are in the world.
¹⁰ But the God of all grace, who hath called us unto his eternal glory by Christ Jesus, after that ye have suffered a while, make you perfect, stablish, strengthen, settle you.

47. I DID SOME THINGS IN MY LIFE I'M SO ASHAMED TO TALK ABOUT. I FEEL I'M NOT WORTHY OF GOD'S FORGIVENESS. WILL HE FORGIVE SUCH HORRID SINS?

To be honest with you, none of us are worthy of God's forgiveness. Nevertheless, He continues to demonstrate His love to us while we remain in our sins. His grace meets us in our pitiful state of being and yet He continues to offer us His redemption. His beautiful gift of "G-R-A-C-E" is: **G**od's **R**edemption **A**t **C**hrist **E**xpense. When we repent of our sins and believe in Christ Jesus, our sins are truly forgiven. Christ died a horrible death on Calvary's cross for us to be free from our past faults and failures. Praise Jesus!

Lastly, I found out through my horrible sins that God is truly merciful. Time after time, He has used what the devil meant for bad, for our good. This is how He uses our mess for our messages in ministry.

> Psalm 103:10-13 (TLB)
> ^{10} He has not punished us as we deserve for all our sins,
> ^{11} for his mercy toward those who fear and honor him is as great as the height of the heavens above the earth.
> ^{12} He has removed our sins as far away from us as the east is from the west.
> ^{13} He is like a father to us, tender and sympathetic to those who reverence him.
>
> Isaiah 55:6-7 (KJV)
> ^{6} Seek ye the LORD while he may be found, call ye upon him while he is near:
> ^{7} Let the wicked forsake his way, and the unrighteous man his thoughts: and let him return unto the LORD, and he will have mercy upon him; and to our God, for he will abundantly pardon.
>
> Matthew 11:28 (KJV)
> Come unto me, all ye that labour and are heavy laden, and I will give you rest.

John 3:16-17 (AMP)
16 For God so greatly loved and dearly prized the world that He [even] gave up His only begotten (unique) Son, so that whoever believes in (trusts in, clings to, relies on) Him shall not perish (come to destruction, be lost) but have eternal (everlasting) life.
17 For God did not send the Son into the world in order to judge (to reject, to condemn, to pass sentence on) the world, but that the world might find salvation and be made safe and sound through Him.

1 John 1: 9 (KJV)
If we confess our sins, he is faithful and just to forgive us our sins, and to cleanse us from all unrighteousness.

48. WHY DOES SOME INDIVIDUALS SAY, "HOMOSEXUAL HEALING DID NOT WORK FOR THEM"?

There are many reasons why individuals believe homosexual healing did not work for them. However, freedom is a choice. These are some reasons why individuals believe their healing did not work:

- Deception
- Discouragements
- Lack of Commitment
- Lack of Faith
- Peer Pressure
- Temptations
- Unbelief

Intimacy

I have witnessed homosexual healing prevailing when there were:

- Christian Fellowship
- Continuous Prayer
- Determination with Commitment
- Exercised Faith
- Self-Denial of Temptations
- Firm Accountability

Matthew 12:43-45 also Luke 11:24-26 (KJV)
Jesus said: [43] When the unclean spirit is gone out of a man, he walketh through dry places, seeking rest, and findeth none.
[44] Then he saith, I will return into my house from whence I came out; and when he is come, he findeth it empty, swept, and garnished.
[45] Then goeth he, and taketh with himself seven other spirits more wicked than himself, and they enter in and dwell there: and the last state of that man is worse than the first. Even so shall it be also unto this wicked generation.

Ephesians 4:14-18 (TLB)
[14] Then we will no longer be like children, forever changing our minds about what we believe because someone has told us something different or has cleverly lied to us and made the lie sound like the truth.
[15-16] Instead, we will lovingly follow the truth at all times—speaking truly, dealing truly, living truly—and so become more and more in every way like Christ who is the Head of his body, the Church. Under his direction, the whole body is fitted together perfectly, and each part in its own special way helps the other parts, so that the

whole body is healthy and growing and full of love.

¹⁷⁻¹⁸ Let me say this, then, speaking for the Lord: Live no longer as the unsaved do, for they are blinded and confused. Their closed hearts are full of darkness; they are far away from the life of God because they have shut their minds against him, and they cannot understand his ways.

2 Peter 2:20-22 (NIV)

²⁰ If they have escaped the corruption of the world by knowing our Lord and Savior Jesus Christ and are again entangled in it and are overcome, they are worse off at the end than they were at the beginning.

²¹ It would have been better for them not to have known the way of righteousness, than to have known it and then to turn their backs on the sacred command that was passed on to them.

²² Of them the proverbs are true: "A dog returns to its vomit," and, "A sow that is washed returns to her wallowing in the mud."

49. IS MASTURBATION A SIN?

Masturbation isn't directly mentioned in the Bible, nevertheless sexual sins are included. Any sex outside of holy matrimony (God's ordained marriage union for a man and a woman) is sin. In time, it opens up so many other areas of lust, perversions and areas in the demonic realm (please see previous answers for questions 42 and 43 in this book). Therefore, in the absence of it being directly mentioned, exercising caution is best. Know that, taking this freedom for liberty will eventually be dangerous and damaging.

Romans 13:14 (AMP)
But clothe yourself with the Lord Jesus Christ (the Messiah), and make no provision for [indulging] the flesh [put a stop to thinking about the evil cravings of your physical nature] to [gratify its] desires (lusts).

1 Corinthians 6:18-20 (AMP)
[18] Shun immorality and all sexual looseness [flee from impurity in thought, word, or deed]. Any other sin which a man commits is one outside the body, but he who commits sexual immorality sins against his own body.
[19] Do you not know that your body is the temple (the very sanctuary) of the Holy Spirit Who lives within you, Whom you have received [as a Gift] from God? You are not your own,
[20] You were bought with a price [purchased with a preciousness and paid for, made His own]. So then, honor God and bring glory to Him in your body.

Galatians 5:16-17 (NLT)
[16] So I say, let the Holy Spirit guide your lives. Then you won't be doing what your sinful nature craves.
[17] The sinful nature wants to do evil, which is just the opposite of what the Spirit wants. And the Spirit gives us desires that are the opposite of what the sinful nature desires. These two forces are constantly fighting each other, so you are not free to carry out your good intentions.

1 Thessalonians 4:3-5 (AMP)
³ For this is the will of God, that you should be consecrated (separated and set apart for pure and holy living): that you should abstain *and* shrink from all sexual vice,
⁴ That each one of you should know how to possess (control, manage) his own body in consecration (purity, separated from things profane) and honor,
⁵ Not [to be used] in the passion of lust like the heathen, who are ignorant of the true God *and* have no knowledge of His will,

James 1:13-15 (NLT)
13 And remember, when you are being tempted, do not say, "God is tempting me." God is never tempted to do wrong, and he never tempts anyone else.
14 Temptation comes from our own desires, which entice us and drag us away.
15 These desires give birth to sinful actions. And when sin is allowed to grow, it gives birth to death.

1 Peter 5:8 (AMP)
Be well balanced (temperate, sober of mind), be vigilant and cautious at all times; for that enemy of yours, the devil, roams around like a lion roaring [in fierce hunger], seeking someone to seize upon and devour.

Relational Lies -

Deception, Deceivers & being Deceived

If deception and lies are part of any relationship, the relationship is in serious trouble. Dishonesty is the opposite of truth, and truth is the enemy to deception. Relational lies conceived in the heart, brings forth deception, and deception give birth to deceivers, and deceivers are TRUTH enemies.

> 2 Timothy 3:13 (KJV)
> But evil men and seducers shall wax worse and worse, deceiving, and being deceived.

---
50. Since God created us, are we all God's children?

Unfortunately, this cliché isn't true. The deception of this suggests that individuals do not have to accept God's Son to become a part of His family. Most people use this cliché because they do not want individuals to feel uncomfortable and/or want to use a statement that is all inclusive. Please do not be deceived; this is not what the bible says. In St. John 8:42-44, Jesus explained: *"If you love Him than God is your Father, but He also stated that some have another father and he is the devil."* Yes, that may sound harsh, but He desires that you *know the truth because it will make you free.*

We are all God's creations, but not all God's children. However, God desire for all of His created beings to be a part of His family. According to 1Timothy 2:4, *"God desires all people to be saved and come into the knowledge of His truth."* Also, 2 Peter 3:9 tells us, *"God do not want anyone to perish, but everyone to come to repentance."*

So, the bible clearly tells us who God's children are. If you have not made this decision yet, please accept God's way and become His son or daughter today. If you do, welcome my brother and welcome my sister to the family of our heavenly Father!

Matthew 5:9 (KJV)
Blessed are the peacemakers: for they shall be called the children of God.

John 1:11-12 (ASV)
[11] He came unto his own, and they that were his own received him not.
[12] But as many as received him, to them gave he the right to become children of God, even to them that believe on his name:

John 8:32 (KJV)
And ye shall know the truth, and the truth shall make you free.

John 8:42-44 (KJV)
[42] Jesus said unto them, If God were your Father, ye would love me: for I proceeded forth and came from God; neither came I of myself, but he sent me.

⁴³ Why do ye not understand my speech? even because ye cannot hear my word.
⁴⁴ Ye are of your father the devil, and the lusts of your father ye will do. He was a murderer from the beginning, and abode not in the truth, because there is no truth in him. When he speaketh a lie, he speaketh of his own: for he is a liar, and the father of it.

Romans 8:14-17 (KJV)
¹⁴ For as many as are led by the Spirit of God, they are the sons of God.
¹⁵ For ye have not received the spirit of bondage again to fear; but ye have received the Spirit of adoption, whereby we cry, Abba, Father.
¹⁶ The Spirit itself beareth witness with our spirit, that we are the children of God:
¹⁷ And if children, then heirs; heirs of God, and joint-heirs with Christ; if so be that we suffer with him, that we may be also glorified together.

1 John 3:10 (KJV)
In this the children of God are manifest, and the children of the devil: whosoever doeth not righteousness is not of God, neither he that loveth not his brother.

51. I KEEP ENCOURAGING MY FRIEND TO GET HELP. CAN YOU GIVE AN EXAMPLE OF WHAT LONG TERM EFFECTS OF SEXUAL ABUSE COULD BE?

The issue your friend maybe experiencing is a phrase many individuals heard growing up. *"What goes on in our family, stays in our family."* According to Revelations 12:11, we disable satan's strongholds when we allow Christ to wash away the pain, guilt or shame. The key to the overcoming satan is the words of our testimonies of healing and freedom through the blood of Christ Jesus. As we share our testimonies with others, this demonstrates God's power; so other individuals can know they too can be set free.

The long-term effects of sexual abuse could be roots of bitterness, low self-esteem, no self-worth, feelings of uncleanness, feelings of hopelessness, shame, fear, anxiety, feelings of inadequacy, suicidal thoughts, anger, violence, incarceration, mental health complications, sexual perversion and this list could go on.

Sexual abuse is a serious problem throughout this world. There are people of all ages who are victims of this sin. Many have not received the help that is needed due to their silence, fear and sometime serious threats from the predator. If you are a victim, you should speak out to a professional person or a mature person you can trust. That way, you can receive the support and help needed to begin the process of healing and wholeness.

> Revelation 12:11 (ASV)
> And they overcame him because of the blood of the Lamb, and because of the word of their testimony; and they loved not their life even unto death.

<u>This is an example in the Bible of damaging effects from sexual abuse within a family</u>:

In historical biblical time, Prince Amnon the first born son of King David fell in love with his half-sister Tamar, the beautiful sister of Prince Absalom, another son of King David. Amnon became so obsessed with his half-sister Tamar, that he became lovesick over her. Tamar was a virgin, therefore was available to marry, but a half-brother and a half-sister was prohibited.

Prince Amnon had a cousin who was his adviser as well, named Jonadab (an evil man who gave him bad advice). He advised Amnon to go to bed and pretend he was sick, then ask his father, King David, if his sister could serve and feed him, so he could feel better. King David agreed and sent word for Tamar to comply. So Tamar obeyed her father's command and went to serve and feed her brother Amnon (2 Samuel 13:1-8).

He plotted to rape Tamar, in the absence of his servants while they were alone. She begged him not to do this horrid act. She was willing to ask their father if her half-brother could legally marry her; but he refused to listen and forced himself to rape her anyway (2 Samuel 13:9-14).

After this despicable act, Prince Absalom put a hit on his brother Prince Amnon, then waited two years and had his servant to kill him. This family was in such disarray over this sin for many years. Which eventually, led to the death of Prince Absalom rebelling against his father King David (2 Samuel 13:15 - 2 Samuel 18:33).

52. I HEARD, "THERE ARE LESBIANS WHO HAVE IMPREGNATED ONE ANOTHER," IS THIS TRUE AND WOULD GOD ALLOW THIS?

Yes, this is true and yes, God has allowed this. My husband and I were trained ministry volunteers at a very busy prolife pregnancy center and learned this is true. There are many public reports confirming females became pregnant through artificial insemination from their female partner. One female would inject sperm into her partner's womb and she actually became pregnant.

Some people may say; this information is giving the devil ammunition. After living in a lesbian lifestyle for so many years, trust me this is no new news to the homosexual community. But please don't be deceived to think, since God allowed this behavior this speaks to His agreement with it.

God's love, mercy and grace are so rich we just cannot comprehend it. His allowing two willing individuals to bring life is only something He could do. This demonstrations that God shows no partialities; if He allowed two unmarried heterosexuals to have babies, than the same is for homosexuals too. This proves that God doesn't categorize sins. In His eyes, there isn't one group of sinners worse than another. This is God's way of demonstrating His love for all people equally; loving sinners, but not the sin.

No one knows the complete plan of God. But know this; He can bless that child to find the cure for cancer or have a world revival to bring millions of souls to Christ. According to Jeremiah 29:11, *He knows the thoughts/plans* why He produced that infant's life!

> Isaiah 55:8-9 (KJV)
> [8] For my thoughts are not your thoughts, neither are your ways my ways, saith the Lord.
> [9] For as the heavens are higher than the earth, so are my ways higher than your ways, and my thoughts than your thoughts.

Jeremiah 29:11 (KJV)
For I know the thoughts that I think toward you, saith the Lord, thoughts of peace, and not of evil, to give you an expected end.

Matthew 5:45 (KJV)
That ye may be the children of your Father which is in heaven: for he maketh his sun to rise on the evil and on the good, and sendeth rain on the just and on the unjust.

Romans 5:8 (KJV)
But God commendeth his love toward us, in that, while we were yet sinners, Christ died for us.

Acts 10:34 also Romans 2:11 (NLT)
Then Peter replied, "I see very clearly that God shows no favoritism.

53. SHOULD CHRISTIANS OPPOSE GAY MARRIAGE AND GAY RELATIONSHIPS?

Christians should agree with what God says in His Holy Word. We should love what God loves which are ways to live in holiness, righteousness and truth. Then we should hate what God hates which are actions of sin and anything that is against His holiness (hating sin, not the sinner).

Everyone is required to give an account to God of their own lives, deeds and choices. This is the very reason God will hold each of us responsible for what we do with our own lives, deeds and choices. So don't be deceived to follow how the majority may agree. Each of us is accountable for our own actions.

Psalm 97:10 (KJV)
Ye that love the LORD, hate evil: he preserveth the souls of his saints; he delivereth them out of the hand of the wicked.

Amos 3:3 (KJV)
Can two walk together, except they be agreed?

Acts 5:29 (KJV)
Then Peter and the other apostles answered and said, We ought to obey God rather than men.

Romans 1:26-27 & 32 (TLB)
[26] That is why God let go of them and let them do all these evil things, so that even their women turned against God's natural plan for them and indulged in sex sin with each other.
[27] And the men, instead of having normal sex relationships with women, burned with lust for each other, men doing shameful things with other men and, as a result, getting paid within their own souls with the penalty they so richly deserved.

[32] They were fully aware of God's death penalty for these crimes, yet they went right ahead and did them anyway and encouraged others to do them, too.

Colossians 2:8 (TLB)
Don't let others spoil your faith and joy with their philosophies, their wrong and shallow answers built on men's thoughts and ideas, instead of on what Christ has said.

John 15:18-19 (KJV)
[18] If the world hate you, ye know that it hated me before it hated you.

¹⁹ If ye were of the world, the world would love his own: but because ye are not of the world, but I have chosen you out of the world, therefore the world hateth you.

---

54. WHAT DO I DO WITH THE FEELINGS OF CONDEMNATION AND SHAME WHEN I MAY HAVE ENJOYED THE FEELINGS FROM AN ACT OF SEXUAL ABUSE (LIKE MOLESTATION, INCEST OR RAPE)?

God created sex for procreation and pleasure between a husband and wife. He created this beautiful and pleasurable sexual experience for us to only enjoy in Holy matrimony. However, pleasure can still be experienced due to the nature of human touch.

Since you have experienced sexual abuse, you are in need of emotional and spiritual cleansing in your soul and spirit. This takes place through you forgiving the predator and repentance of your sins. After this, the condemnation and shame will began to pass away. Support groups, therapy, and counseling would also be helpful in this healing process.

Additionally, the results of ungodly sexual acts may cause damage overtime to the body, soul and spirit since it is against God's Holy standards. Because sex sells and generates billions of dollars in revenue, many innocent individuals have become its victims through molestation, incest or rape.

These dangerous and damaging results are due to glamorized sex which include pornography, advertisements, music lyrics, and peer pressure. Therefore, the devil has perverted it into a beast of destruction and this devastation. This can eventually bring unbearable pain without receiving complete healing and deliverance. Jesus paid a dear price for this freedom; therefore ask Him, receive it and be healed in Jesus name!

> Genesis 2:24, Matthew 19:5, Mark 10:7 also Ephesians 5:31 (KJV)
> Therefore shall a man leave his father and his mother, and shall cleave unto his wife: and they shall be one flesh.
>
> Psalms 37:5 (KJV)
> Commit thy way unto the Lord; trust also in him; and he shall bring it to pass.
>
> Isaiah 53:4-5 (KJV)
> [4] Surely he hath borne our griefs, and carried our sorrows: yet we did esteem him stricken, smitten of God, and afflicted.
> [5] But he was wounded for our transgressions, he was bruised for our iniquities: the chastisement of our peace was upon him; and with his stripes we are healed.
>
> Romans 8:1-4 (KJV)
> [1] There is therefore now no condemnation to them which are in Christ Jesus, who walk not after the flesh, but after the Spirit.
> [2] For the law of the Spirit of life in Christ Jesus hath made me free from the law of sin and death.
> [3] For what the law could not do, in that it was weak through the flesh, God sending his own Son in the likeness of sinful flesh, and for sin, condemned sin in the flesh:

⁴ That the righteousness of the law might be fulfilled in us, who walk not after the flesh, but after the Spirit.

Galatians 5:1 (KJV)
Stand fast therefore in the liberty wherewith Christ hath made us free, and be not entangled again with the yoke of bondage.

1 John 3:20 (KJV)
For if our heart condemn us, God is greater than our heart, and knoweth all things.

55. HOW DO YOU OVERCOME THE THOUGHTS OF SUICIDE?

Seek medical attention and/or call the suicide crises hotline immediately. They are trained professionals that can assist to sort out physical and mental situations.

On the other hand, no one can do this in their own strength especially without God's help. The devil, who desires to kill, steal and destroy your life, has been at this same evil act way too long to fight against him in your own strength.

Open up to someone and do not try to handle this on your own. Think of your loved ones that will be left behind to grieve your death and bear this pain. Maybe you are too close to the problem to see the beautiful rainbow ahead for your life. Season change, this may be your winter or rainy season (problems pouring in all at once); but your springtime is on its way. This is a good time to allow a loved one, a positive close friend, a mentor, a teacher, a minister, a policeman and/or a crises hotline staff to help you sort things out.

These are reasons why some individuals has given up and taken their own life. They give in to the devil lies of hopelessness as he whispers; *"No one loves you and who cares if you die"* with deceptions of: *"This is the best choice and there is no other way out."*

I remember one of my suicide attempts, God sent a policeman to speak with me; because my female partner called the authorities for assistance. The officer helped me sort out problems I was going through and he helped me see a bigger picture for my life.

Resisting thoughts of suicide by thinking and speaking scriptures (because God's Word gives life) is a great exercise. Bible passages have power and authority over the devil for these are God-breathed (2 Timothy 3:16-17). His Word will transform your life. You will eventually see how significant and valuable you are to God and why He want you alive. It's not only for you, but for so many other individuals as well.

Psalm 34:17-18 (KJV)
[17] The righteous cry, and the Lord heareth, and delivereth them out of all their troubles.
[18] The Lord is nigh unto them that are of a broken heart; and saveth such as be of a contrite spirit.

Ecclesiastes 7:17(b) (KJV)
: why shouldest thou die before thy time?

Jeremiah 29:11 (KJV)
For I know the thoughts that I think toward you, saith the Lord, thoughts of peace, and not of evil, to give you an expected end.

John 10:10 - (KJV)
Jesus said: The thief cometh not, but for to steal, and to kill, and to destroy: I am come that they might have life, and that they might have it more abundantly.

Romans 12:2 (KJV)
And be not conformed to this world: but be ye transformed by the renewing of your mind, that ye may prove what is that good, and acceptable, and perfect, will of God.

2 Corinthians 10:3-5 (KJV)
³ For though we walk in the flesh, we do not war after the flesh:
⁴ (For the weapons of our warfare are not carnal, but mighty through God to the pulling down of strong holds;)
⁵ Casting down imaginations, and every high thing that exalteth itself against the knowledge of God, and bringing into captivity every thought to the obedience of Christ;

2 Corinthians 12:9 (KJV)
And he said unto me, My grace is sufficient for thee: for my strength is made perfect in weakness. Most gladly therefore will I rather glory in my infirmities, that the power of Christ may rest upon me.

Philippians 4:8 (KJV)
Finally, brethren, whatsoever things are true, whatsoever things are honest, whatsoever things are just, whatsoever things are pure, whatsoever things are lovely, whatsoever things are of good

report; if there be any virtue, and if there be any praise, think on these things.

56. MY FRIENDS ARE IN A COMMITTED AND LOVING RELATIONSHIP FOR YEARS NOW. WHAT IS THE BIG DEAL THAT THEY ARE NOT MARRIED?

According to most dictionaries; *Cohabitation is an arrangement where two individuals who are not married and live together. Through this arrangement, they are emotionally and/or sexually involved.* According to this definition, this arrangement is clearly against God's directions for intimate relationships. His desire for cohabitation is strictly for a man and a woman to come together in holy matrimony; so He can bless their commitment in marriage. Also according to the bible, cohabiting outside of marriage is fornication.

My plea for individuals who find themselves at this point in a cohabitating arrangement, please reconsider your lifestyle to reflect God's way. He will only bless lifestyles that reveal His righteousness and holiness. He is absolutely Holy and cannot go against His commandments to suit human desires and lifestyles. You may have the finest things in life, but don't be deceived by the devil that these are God's blessings. Your soul is precious and worth much more than things.

Genesis 2:24, Matthew 19:5, Mark 10:7 also Ephesians 5:31 (KJV)
Therefore shall a man leave his father and his mother, and shall cleave unto his wife: and they shall be one flesh.

John 14:15 (AMP)
Jesus said: If you [really] love Me, you will keep (obey) My commands.

1 Corinthians 7:2 (KJV)
Nevertheless, to avoid fornication, let every man have his own wife, and let every woman have her own husband.

1 John 4:9-10 (TLB)
⁹ God showed how much he loved us by sending his only Son into this wicked world to bring to us eternal life through his death.
¹⁰ In this act we see what real love is: it is not our love for God but his love for us when he sent his Son to satisfy God's anger against our sins.

1 Corinthians 6:18 (KJV)
Flee fornication. Every sin that a man doeth is without the body; but he that committeth fornication sinneth against his own body.

Hebrews 13:4 (ASV)
Let marriage be had in honor among all, and let the bed be undefiled: for fornicators and adulterers God will judge.

CHILDHOOD ABUSE – I WAS ONLY A CHILD - Y' ME?

Childhood abuse is a global epidemic. There are countless individuals across America, and throughout the world that have not received help nor healing of childhood abuse. Throughout the world, there are heightened statistics in divorces, domestic violence, crime, incarceration, mental illness and other dysfunctional behaviors from the unfortunate root of childhood abuse. Untreated abuse is very painful and damaging to the soul. There is help, start today; because you are worth it. Jesus paid a high price for you to be free!

57. WHY DO SOME ADULTS USE THEIR AUTHORITY TO TAKE ADVANTAGE OF A CHILD? "WHY ME?"

I am very sorry that you have experienced this horrible act of abuse.

Hurting people hurt other people, which cause deep pain. There are some unhealthy individuals in this world that need more help than others. But unfortunately, they do not seek the proper help that is needed. These unhealthy individuals need much prayer and a lot of professional assistance. However, you choosing to forgive him or her in your heart will be a way to start your healing process.

Later, you may see how God can use your bad experience to help others overcome their abusive experiences. Just remember, according to Genesis 50:20, *"What the devil meant for bad, God can use it for good."*

> Genesis 50:20 (NLT)
> You intended to harm me, but God intended it all for good. He brought me to this position so I could save the lives of many people.
>
> Proverbs 15:3 (KJV)
> The eyes of the LORD are in every place, beholding the evil and the good.
>
> Psalms 126:5 (KJV)
> They that sow in tears shall reap in joy.
>
> Isaiah 54:4 (NLT)
> "Fear not; you will no longer live in shame. Don't be afraid; there is no more disgrace for you. You will no longer remember the shame of your youth and the sorrows of widowhood.
>
> Jeremiah 29:11 (KJV)
> For I know the thoughts that I think toward you, saith the Lord, thoughts of peace, and not of evil, to give you an expected end.

John 5:6 (KJV)
When Jesus saw him lie, and knew that he had been now a long time *in that case*, he saith unto him, Wilt thou be made whole?

---

58. MY FIANCÉ RESPECTS ME AS A STRONG MAN OF GOD; BUT I SOMETIME DEAL WITH LOW SELF-ESTEEM, THINKING ABOUT BEING RAPED BY A FEMALE AS A YOUTH. SHOULD I SHARE THIS WITH HER PRIOR TO OUR WEDDING?

Please seek counseling before getting married. This was an unpleasant experience and being honest within yourself will bring healing. Doing this prior to marriage is best. Privately ask your counselor, when is an appropriate time during these sessions to share this sensitive information. Maybe this confession will be a start of your healing process. Also, if you feel you need additional counseling prior to marriage, now is the best time to consider receiving it.

In other words, this would resemble holding a volley ball in a bucket under water for a long period of time. Unfortunately when your arms become weary of holding it, the ball will surface abruptly! (The ball represents your physical abuse). This could be very damaging to you and your relationship.

Without healing, some of the "fruit affects" are anger, anxiety, substance abuse, relational withdrawals, weight issues (bulimia or obesity), infidelity, unknown triggers and so much more. This occurs when individuals wait too long to seek help or try to suppress the pain. Unfortunately, their love-ones have no idea of "the root" cause.

You are becoming one with your wife to be and she should be the one you share all of your secrets, hurts, failures and hang-ups. There are many adventures and other work to do in marriage that will need your undivided attention. Therefore, going into marriage healed and whole is best for a wonderful new beginning.

Isaiah 41:10 (KJV)
Fear thou not; for I am with thee: be not dismayed; for I am thy God: I will strengthen thee; yea, I will help thee; yea, I will uphold thee with the right hand of my righteousness.

Isaiah 61:7 (NIV)
Instead of your shame you will receive a double portion, and instead of disgrace you will rejoice in your inheritance. And so you will inherit a double portion in your land, and everlasting joy will be yours.

Zephaniah 3:19 (NIV)
At that time I will deal with all who oppressed you. I will rescue the lame; I will gather the exiles. I will give them praise and honor in every land where they have suffered shame.

Galatians 5:1(a) (TLB)
So Christ has made us free. Now make sure that you stay free

Ephesians 4:15(a) (AMP)
Rather, let our lives lovingly express truth [in all things, speaking truly, dealing truly, living truly].

Jude 1:20 (KJV)
[20] But ye, beloved, building up yourselves on your most holy faith, praying in the Holy Ghost,

59. I WAS MOLESTED AS A BOY, SHOULD I SHARE THIS WITH MY WIFE?

Marriage is a partnership and we should be able to tell our spouse everything about ourselves; the Bible tells us *"we are one"* (Matthew 19:6). Honesty is the best policy for wholeness, healing and freedom. Unfortunately this is something that should have come out in premarital counseling. So since you are asking this question it means you are seeking freedom.

I have witnessed a marriage seriously damaged, because a spouse viewed this negatively. Please seek post-marital counsel if you believe your wife may not receive this information well. Pray for wisdom, read scripture for continuous direction and seek godly guidance. These steps will help you toward the freedom you are seeking.

Psalm 119:105 (KJV)
Thy word *is* a lamp unto my feet, and a light unto my path.

Proverbs 11:14 (KJV)
Where no counsel is, the people fall: but in the multitude of counsellors there is safety.

James 1:5 (NIV)
⁵ If any of you lacks wisdom, you should ask God, who gives generously to all without finding fault, and it will be given to you.

James 5:16 (KJV)
Confess your faults one to another, and pray one for another, that ye may be healed. The effectual fervent prayer of a righteous man availeth much.

---

60. I USE TO BE A HAPPY CHILD AND EVERYBODY WANTED TO BE AROUND ME BECAUSE I WAS FRIENDLY AND FUNNY. NOW I AM IN MY THIRTIES, AN INTROVERT AND I STILL HURT FROM THOSE SEXUAL AND EMOTIONAL SCARS. WHY ME?

I cannot begin to tell you how sorry I am that this unfortunate incident has happened to you. Nor can I tell you why this terrible thing happened to you.

Deep down inside that happy and fun person wants to escape the memory of that abuse and enjoy life again. Please seek counseling to help you walk through the path of this pain and unfortunate experience. An astute counselor or pastor should have ways to guide you to wholeness and healing.

Speak life to yourself through the Word of God; scriptures and phrases such as: "*I can do all things through Christ who strengthens me, I am blessed and not cursed, God loves me and that is good enough for me*".

Another example, I sing the hymn by William Batchelder Bradbury; *Jesus Loves Me* (this keeps me encouraged daily, as I wash my hands clean):

> Jesus loves me—this I know,
> For the Bible tells me so;
> Little ones to Him belong—
> They are weak, but He is strong.
>
> Yes, Jesus loves me!
> Yes, Jesus loves me!
> Yes, Jesus loves me!
> The Bible tells me so.

Then, watch how you will begin to release the pain that is weighing your spirit down. God has given His children power to speak life, so use that power He has invested within you to live again!

> Proverbs 16:3-5 (NIV)
> ³ Commit to the Lord whatever you do, and he will establish your plans.
> ⁴ The Lord works out everything to its proper end— even the wicked for a day of disaster.
> ⁵ The Lord detests all the proud of heart. Be sure of this: They will not go unpunished.
>
> Proverbs 18:21 (AMP)
> Death and life are in the power of the tongue, and they who indulge in it shall eat the fruit of it [for death or life].
>
> 2 Timothy 1:7 (TLB & KJV)
> (TLB) For the Holy Spirit, God's gift, does not want you to be afraid of people, but to be wise and strong, and to love them and enjoy being with
>
> 1 Peter 5:7 (KJV)
> Casting all your care upon him; for he careth for you.

THE SIGNS OF THE TIME – MY WAY OR GOD'S WAY

Jesus informed His disciples that the world was coming to an end and He was going to return back to the earth to receive them. But there would be events that would occur before his return; these events are referred to as *"The Second coming of Christ"*, *"The Last Hour"*, *Christ's Return"*, *"End-Time"*, *"The Rapture"*, etc.

Individuals plan months and years for a vacation. They buy life insurance, but what about plans or insurance after this life? Will you be ready?

---

61. DOES THE SAME-SEX MARRIAGE AGENDA SHOW ANY SIGNS OF END TIME PROPHECIES CONCERNING JESUS' RETURN TO THE EARTH?

Absolutely. We can see how people are ignoring morals and values that most people just a few years ago wouldn't tolerate (rudeness, nudity, perversion, violence, same-sex marriage and the list could go on...). So as Jesus mentioned in Luke 17:25-30; *"He would be rejected while people would be enjoying themselves partying, getting married"* and so on, until

His return. I can clearly see this happening today. However, the "*getting married*" part in verse 27, really caught my attention the most. We see how the same-sex marriage agenda is on the rise. People are now having same-sex marriages and are being given in same-sex marriages, which we have never seen or heard of in the past!

Even the Apostle Paul warned us in these scriptures - 2 Thessalonians 2:3 and 1 Timothy 4:1; of "*a great falling away of individuals who professed to be Christians.*" We see a great number of individuals lately, following after sin and agreeing with same-sex marriage and the homosexual agenda.

Luke 17:25-30 (TLB)
Jesus said: ^{25} But first I must suffer terribly and be rejected by this whole nation.
^{26} "When I return the world will be as indifferent to the things of God* as the people were in Noah's day.
^{27} They ate and drank and married—everything just as usual right up to the day when Noah went into the ark and the Flood came and destroyed them all.
^{28} "And the world will be as it was in the days of Lot: people went about their daily business—eating and drinking, buying and selling, farming and building—
^{29} until the morning Lot left Sodom. Then fire and brimstone rained down from heaven and destroyed them all.
^{30} Yes, it will be 'business as usual' right up to the hour of my return.

2 Thessalonians 2:3 (AMP)
Let no one deceive *or* beguile you in any way, for that day will not come except the apostasy comes first [unless the predicted great falling away of those who have professed to be Christians has come], and the man of lawlessness (sin) is revealed, who is the son of doom (of perdition),

1 Timothy 4:1-2 (TLB)
¹ But the Holy Spirit tells us clearly that in the last times some in the church will turn away from Christ and become eager followers of teachers with devil-inspired ideas.
² These teachers will tell lies with straight faces and do it so often that their consciences won't even bother them.

2 Timothy 3:1-5 (TLB)
¹ You may as well know this too, Timothy, that in the last days it is going to be very difficult to be a Christian.
² For people will love only themselves and their money; they will be proud and boastful, sneering at God, disobedient to their parents, ungrateful to them, and thoroughly bad.
³ They will be hardheaded and never give in to others; they will be constant liars and troublemakers and will think nothing of immorality. They will be rough and cruel, and sneer at those who try to be good.
⁴ They will betray their friends; they will be hotheaded, puffed up with pride, and prefer good times to worshiping God.
⁵ They will go to church, yes, but they won't really believe anything they hear. Don't be taken in by people like that.

62. IS HELL REAL AND AS BAD AS PEOPLE SAY?

Hell is very real. It is a place of eternal suffering, torment, hopelessness and rejection. Because our minds cannot comprehend the full deity of God, it is difficult for some individuals to believe that He will allow a person to make this choice for their final eternal destination. However, He has given us the bible, many resources, and other individuals to share His message about eternity. Some people believe if they would just ignore the warnings of God's wrath and eternity, then it will all be okay; but an eternal destination is inevitable.

The bible says, "*Hell was created for satan and his falling angels.*" Individuals who refuse to accept truth and rebel against God; unfortunately they will inherit the same punishment. The bible also says in Isaiah 5:14, "*Hell has enlarged itself*" and this has happened because individuals have purposed in their heart that they will reject God's way as satan and the falling angels have done.

In these scriptures, Jesus have revealed that everyone in Hell will have their five senses; "*sight, touch, smell, hearing and taste*". Hell is not an imaginary place; it is real and currently many people are there waiting for the final judgment day:

> Luke 16:23-28 (KJV)
> **_Jesus said_**: [23] And in hell he lift up his eyes, being in torments, and seeth Abraham afar off, and Lazarus in his bosom.
> [24] And he cried and said, Father Abraham, have mercy on me, and send Lazarus, that he may dip the tip of his finger in water, and cool my tongue; for I am tormented in this flame.

²⁵ But Abraham said, Son, <u>remember</u> that thou in thy lifetime receivedst thy good things, and likewise Lazarus evil things: but now he is comforted, and <u>thou art tormented</u>.
²⁶ And beside all this, <u>between us</u> and you there is a great gulf fixed: so that they which would pass from hence to you cannot; neither can they pass to us, that would come from thence.
²⁷ Then he said, <u>I pray thee</u> therefore, father, that thou wouldest send him to my father's house:
²⁸ For I have five brethren; that he may testify unto them, lest they also come into this <u>place of torment</u>.

Lastly, it does not matter what people say since we have facts through the Holy Bible and these are a few of those scriptures:

Isaiah 5:14 (KJV)
Therefore hell hath enlarged herself, and opened her mouth without measure: and their glory, and their multitude, and their pomp, and he that rejoiceth, shall descend into it.

Isaiah 14:9-11 (KJV)
⁹ Hell from beneath is moved for thee to meet thee at thy coming: it stirreth up the dead for thee, even all the chief ones of the earth; it hath raised up from their thrones all the kings of the nations.
¹⁰ All they shall speak and say unto thee, Art thou also become weak as we? art thou become like unto us?
¹¹ Thy pomp is brought down to the grave, and the noise of thy viols: the worm is spread under thee, and the worms cover thee.

Isaiah 66:24 (NLT)
And as they go out, they will see the dead bodies of those who have rebelled against me. For the worms that devour them will never die, and the fire that burns them will never go out. All who pass by will view them with utter horror."

Matthew 25:41 (KJV)
Jesus said: Then shall he say also unto them on the left hand, Depart from me, ye cursed, into everlasting fire, prepared for the devil and his angels:

Mark 9:47(b)- 49(a) (KJV)
Jesus said: 47(b)- to be cast into hell fire:
^{48} Where their worm dieth not, and the fire is not quenched
$^{49(a)}$ For every one shall be salted with fire,

Hebrews 9:27-28 (KJV)
^{27} And as it is <u>appointed unto men once to die, but after this the judgment</u>:
^{28} So Christ was once offered to bear the sins of many; and unto them that look for him shall he appear the second time without sin unto salvation.

Jude 1:7 (TLB)
And don't forget the cities of Sodom and Gomorrah and their neighboring towns, all full of lust of every kind, including lust of men for other men. Those cities were destroyed by fire and continue to be a <u>warning to us that there is a hell in which sinners are punished</u>.

63. Since God is a Loving God, will He really send someone to Hell?

God does not choose or desire for anyone to go to Hell. Since Hell was not created for humans; it was created for satan and the fallen angels. When we choose or reject Jesus as our Savior this decision determines our final destination after life on earth. When individuals continue to willfully sin, it shows that they chose satan instead of choosing God, according to 1 John 3:8.

The lies that satan tell individuals are, "*Hell isn't real and a loving God would not send anyone there.*" A part of this is correct, God does not send anyone to Hell; we chose our final destination. According to 1 Peter 2:4, God being impartial allowed the angles to choose Hell as their final destination. He did not give these angels a pass; their own decision led them to Hell.

Please notice Romans 6:23; *"the wages of sin is death"* are the earnings received from making the decision of rejecting Christ. Then, *"the gift of God through Christ is eternal life"* the reward is eternal life in heaven, not eternal Hell.

A sad reality is: everyone currently in Hell is now a believer, but it is too late!

I plead with you; please accept His gift of eternal life today!

Deuteronomy 4:24 also Hebrews 12:29 (KJV)
For the LORD thy God is a consuming fire, even a jealous God.

Romans 6:23 (KJV)
For the wages of sin is death; but the gift of God is eternal life through Jesus Christ our Lord.

James 2:19 (KJV)
Thou believest that there is one God; thou doest well: the devils also believe, and tremble.

1 Peter 2:4-10 (NLT)
⁴ For God did not spare even the angels who sinned. He threw them into hell, in gloomy pits of darkness, where they are being held until the day of judgment.
⁵ And God did not spare the ancient world—except for Noah and the seven others in his family. Noah warned the world of God's righteous judgment. So God protected Noah when he destroyed the world of ungodly people with a vast flood.
⁶ Later, God condemned the cities of Sodom and Gomorrah and turned them into heaps of ashes. He made them an example of what will happen to ungodly people.
⁷ But God also rescued Lot out of Sodom because he was a righteous man who was sick of the shameful immorality of the wicked people around him.
⁸ Yes, Lot was a righteous man who was tormented in his soul by the wickedness he saw and heard day after day.
⁹ So you see, the Lord knows how to rescue godly people from their trials, even while keeping the wicked under punishment until the day of final judgment.

¹⁰ He is especially hard on those who follow their own twisted sexual desire, and who despise authority.

2 Peter 3:9 (TLB)
He isn't really being slow about his promised return, even though it sometimes seems that way. But he is waiting, for the good reason that he is not willing that any should perish, and he is giving more time for sinners to repent.

1 John 3:8-9 (TLB)
⁸ But if you keep on sinning, it shows that you belong to Satan, who since he first began to sin has kept steadily at it. But the Son of God came to destroy these works of the devil.
⁹ The person who has been born into God's family does not make a practice of sinning because now God's life is in him; so he can't keep on sinning, for this new life has been born into him and controls him—he has been born again.

Revelation 12:9 (KJV)
And the great dragon was cast out, that old serpent, called the Devil, and Satan, which deceiveth the whole world: he was cast out into the earth, and his angels were cast out with him.

Healed, Now What? -
You can be "Unquestionably Free!"

Being healed from things that had you bound is a wonderful thing, but you must learn how to walk in your freedom. Freedom is a choice and your decision to follow Christ will allow you the blessing of remaining delivered. Jesus said, *"Who the Son set free, is unquestionably free"* (John 8:36-AMP).

> **64. My friends are not bad people and they are fun to be with; they just live a different lifestyle. I accepted Christ and do not live that way anymore. So, what's the big deal?**

God is not against us having fun with our friends. But your unsaved friends will either influence you back into a lifestyle of sin or you will win them to Christ. This choice of trying to win past friendships your way is more challenging than you may think. Your unsaved friends must see your new life in Christ. Please know that this will take some time.

No one likes losing friends because it could be hard work finding new ones, but it is worth it. It is for your good to find new Christian friends, since your old activities with past friends did not glorify God. Trust me; He will reward you for your faithfulness to Him.

Proverbs 11:30 (KJV)
The fruit of the righteous is a tree of life; and he that winneth souls is wise.

Proverbs 18:24 (KJV)
A man *that hath* friends must shew himself friendly: and there is a friend *that* sticketh closer than a brother.

Mark 10:29-30 (KJV)
[29] And Jesus answered and said, Verily I say unto you, There is no man that hath left house, or brethren, or sisters, or father, or mother, or wife, or children, or lands, for my sake, and the gospel's,
[30] But he shall receive an hundredfold now in this time, houses, and brethren, and sisters, and mothers, and children, and lands, with persecutions; and in the world to come eternal life.

James 4:4 (TLB)
You are like an unfaithful wife who loves her husband's enemies. Don't you realize that making friends with God's enemies—the evil pleasures of this world—makes you an enemy of God? I say it again, that if your aim is to enjoy the evil pleasure of the unsaved world, you cannot also be a friend of God.

2 Peter 3:17 (TLB)
I am warning you ahead of time, dear brothers, so that you can watch out and not be carried away by the mistakes of these wicked men, lest you yourselves become mixed up too.

1 John 2:15 (KJV)
Love not the world, neither the things *that are* in the world. If any man love the world, the love of the Father is not in him.

---

65. MY FRIENDS AND I ATTEND A LGBTQ AFFIRMING CHRISTIAN CHURCH. SHOULD I CONTINUE TO ATTEND THIS CHURCH TO HELP THEM FIND THE TRUTH THAT I'VE RECENTLY FOUND?

Now that you have found truth, stay with the new truth you have found. Real truth comes from God's Word; but if you are not lead by His spirit, you can be deceived. Your spiritual eyes have been opened through His truth and the scales of sin have been removed through accepting Jesus as your Savior.

I plead with you to stay on your new path. My suggestion, please find a new church that is teaching the entire gospel truth. Then, invite your former friends to join you. If they refuse, then you have done your best. Your heart is in the right place to want to help your friends who are still lost. Your next step is to put on the whole armor of God, before trying to rescue others prematurely.

Sometimes that is the devil's way to trick individuals of thinking they are doing something for God, but the devil knows they are not strong enough for the batter. Every good thing is not a God thing; we must be led by the Holy Spirit. Continue to pray for those individuals, plant a seed of salvation and watch how God will save them in His timing.

THIS IS WHAT THE UNGODLY DO:

Matthew 15:8 (KJV)
This people draweth nigh unto fme with their mouth, and honoureth me with their lips; but their heart is far from me.

Romans 1:25 (KJV)
Who changed the truth of God into a lie, and worshipped and served the creature more than the Creator, who is blessed for ever. Amen.

Romans 6:17-18 (NIV)
[17] I urge you, brothers and sisters, to watch out for those who cause divisions and put obstacles in your way that are contrary to the teaching you have learned. Keep away from them.
[18] For such people are not serving our Lord Christ, but their own appetites. By smooth talk and flattery they deceive the minds of naive people.

1 Corinthians 15:33 (AMP)
Do not be so deceived and misled! Evil companionships (communion, associations) corrupt and deprave good manners and morals and character.

1 Timothy 4:1-2 (TLB)
[1] But the Holy Spirit tells us clearly that in the last times some in the church will turn away from Christ and become eager followers of teachers with devil-inspired ideas.
[2] These teachers will tell lies with straight faces and do it so often that their consciences won't even bother them.

2 Timothy 3:13 (TLB)
In fact, evil men and false teachers will become worse and worse, deceiving many, they themselves having been deceived by Satan.

2 Timothy 4:3-4 (NIV)
³ For the time will come when people will not put up with sound doctrine. Instead, to suit their own desires, they will gather around them a great number of teachers to say what their itching ears want to hear.
⁴ They will turn their ears away from the truth and turn aside to myths.

<u>MY SUGGESTION:</u>
2 Corinthians 5:17 (ASV)
Wherefore if any man is in Christ, he is a new creature: the old things are passed away; behold, they are become new.

2 Corinthians 6:17-18 (ASV)
¹⁷ Wherefore Come ye out from among them, and be ye separate, saith the Lord, And touch no unclean thing; And I will receive you,
¹⁸ And will be to you a Father, And ye shall be to me sons and daughters, saith the Lord Almighty.

Ephesians 6:11-13 (TLB)
¹¹ Put on all of God's armor so that you will be able to stand safe against all strategies and tricks of Satan.
¹² For we are not fighting against people made of flesh and blood, but against persons without bodies—the evil rulers of the unseen world, those mighty satanic beings and great evil princes of

darkness who rule this world; and against huge numbers of wicked spirits in the spirit world.
¹³ So use every piece of God's armor to resist the enemy whenever he attacks, and when it is all over, you will still be standing up.

Philippians 3:3 (KJV)
For we are the circumcision, which worship God in the spirit, and rejoice in Christ Jesus, and have no confidence in the flesh.

66. HOW DO I WITNESS THE GOSPEL OF JESUS CHRIST TO MY PAST HOMOSEXUAL FRIENDS?

It is imperative to use God's Word, not human theology. According to John 14:6, Jesus teaches He is: **the way** (to God), **the truth** (God's Word) and **the life** (God's plan). Witnessing to a homosexual person is no different in witnessing to anyone else. God do not categorize sin, sin is sin. <u>Every sinner</u> must accept Jesus Christ as their Lord and Savior, believe that He paid their sin debt and confess their sins to Him, asking for His forgiveness. Ultimately, live holy. Period!

Lastly, testimonies are a powerful witness, so individuals can see the wonderful works of God and witness scriptures coming alive. Remember the "GOSPEL" is the "GOOD NEWS" of Jesus Christ and His wondrous works!

John 14:6 (KJV)
Jesus saith unto him, I am the way, the truth, and the life: no man cometh unto the Father, but by me.

Romans 10:9-10 (NLT)
^{9} If you confess with your mouth that Jesus is Lord and believe in your heart that God raised him from the dead, you will be saved.
^{10} For it is by believing in your heart that you are made right with God, and it is by confessing with your mouth that you are saved.

1 Corinthians 3:6-7 (ASV)
^{6} I planted, Apollos watered; but God gave the increase.
^{7} So then neither is he that planteth anything, neither he that watereth; but God that giveth the increase.

2 Timothy 3:16 (NLT)
All Scripture is inspired by God and is useful to teach us what is true and to make us realize what is wrong in our lives. It corrects us when we are wrong and teaches us to do what is right.

1 John 3:18 (AMP)
Little children, let us not love [merely] in theory or in speech but in deed and in truth (in practice and in sincerity).

Revelation 12:11 (ASV)
And they overcame him because of the blood of the Lamb, and because of the word of their testimony; and they loved not their life even unto death.

67. HOW DO I FIND THE RIGHT CHURCH?

Pray to God for Him to lead you to a bible believing church that teaches the whole truth about the gospel of Jesus Christ. This should be a church that teaches what God expects of us and how He instructs us to live. Unfortunately there are churches that predominately focus on the blessings and prosperity of God. There is so much more which God requires of us to receive the blessings He has assigned for us.

I think of church in this way: it is like a laundromat. If we take our dirty clothes there, sit around and fellowship, but not put the clothes in the washing machine, then our purpose of going there wasn't accomplished. When we put those dirty clothes (which represent our lives) in the washing machine (Word of God), start it (having faith in God's Word) with cleansing soap (the Blood of Jesus) and water (the Holy Spirit); then the cleansing takes place.

Importantly, the main mechanism inside of the washing machine is "The Agitator" (God's instructions in the Holy Bible). God's Word transforms us to be like Christ and purify us from the inside/out.

The messages maybe funny, the cathedral maybe gorgeous and the people could be sweet as pie; but this is your life. You want to find a church that will challenge you to go to higher levels in Christ. Ask God, where He will use your gifts, talents, anointing and purpose. Seek a church that will teach you to be a true Christian "Christ-like". Therefore, if the teachings of a church do not communicate the entire truth from the bible, you have not found the right church.

Jeremiah 42:3 (KJV)
That the LORD thy God may shew us the way wherein we may walk, and the thing that we may do.

Psalm 92:13 (KJV)
Those that be planted in the house of the LORD shall flourish in the courts of our God.

Psalm 119:105 (KJV)
Thy word *is* a lamp unto my feet, and a light unto my path.

Proverbs 3:5-6 (KJV)
[5] Trust in the Lord with all thine heart; and lean not unto thine own understanding.
[6] In all thy ways acknowledge him, and he shall direct thy paths.

Hebrews 10:25 (NLT)
And let us not neglect our meeting together, as some people do, but encourage one another, especially now that the day of his return is drawing near.

68. WHY DOES IT SEEM TO BE SUCH A STRUGGLE IN TRYING TO LIVE HOLY?

We will always have struggles and battles to fight because we have a real enemy who is the devil/satan that hates us for choosing to live for God. Since we inherited a sinful nature from Adam's disobedience, our flesh will always fight to disagree with the righteousness of Christ in us.

The more we build a personal relationship with Christ, the stronger we become in knowing Him in a more intimate way. We need to seek his strength every day in some kind of way. This could be corporate or private reading and studying His Word. We can worship Him in song, prayer, and fellowship with other Christians, etc.

Serving others in your community that is less fortunate will bring joy and strength as well. This is why Jesus came to serve instead of being served (Matthew 20:28). It is a blessing and a reward in giving.

Nehemiah 8:10b (KJV)
: for this day is holy unto our Lord: neither be ye sorry; for the joy of the LORD is your strength.

Psalm 28:7 (KJV)
The LORD is my strength and my shield; my heart trusted in him, and I am helped: therefore my heart greatly rejoiceth; and with my song will I praise him.

Proverbs 3:5-6 (KJV)
[5] Trust in the Lord with all thine heart; and lean not unto thine own understanding.
[6] In all thy ways acknowledge him, and he shall direct thy paths.

Matthew 11:28 (KJV)
Come unto me, all ye that labour and are heavy laden, and I will give you rest.

Romans 7:21-25 (NLT)
[21] I have discovered this principle of life—that when I want to do what is right, I inevitably do what is wrong.
[22] I love God's law with all my heart.
[23] But there is another power within me that is at war with my mind. This power makes me a slave to the sin that is still within me.
[24] Oh, what a miserable person I am! Who will free me from this life that is dominated by sin and death?
[25] Thank God! The answer is in Jesus Christ our Lord. So you see how it is: In my mind I really want to obey God's law, but because of my sinful nature I am a slave to sin.

1 Corinthians 10:13 (KJV)
There hath no temptation taken you but such as is common to man: but God is faithful, who will not suffer you to be tempted above that ye are able; but will with the temptation also make a way to escape, that ye may be able to bear it.

Jude 1:20-21 (KJV)
[20] But ye, beloved, building up yourselves on your most holy faith, praying in the Holy Ghost,
[21] Keep yourselves in the love of God, looking for the mercy of our Lord Jesus Christ unto eternal life.

> **69. PEOPLE TOLD ME: *"THEY WILL BE HERE FOR ME"*; BUT AFTER A WHILE, I FEEL ALL ALONE. HOW CAN I GET THE STRENGTH TO LIVE THIS NEW LIFE IN CHRIST FROM MY ADDICTIONS?**

Seek compatible Christian support groups that will understand and embrace your type of new lifestyle of healing. Finding groups that support special areas of healing may be your best choice to overcome your past behavior and embrace your new way of life. Then, find <u>strong believers</u> within that circle for accountability. These individuals should be those that are in leadership or has been on their new path for some time that could mentor you.

In addition, I have noticed after several years of journaling, this became therapy that helped me tremendously during some very lonely and difficult times. Journaling will surprise you overtime. You will begin to see your progress after a week, month and year. Your growth in Christ will become much stronger and you will not need the support of others as much. Even King David encouraged himself in the Lord.

> 1 Samuel 30:6 (KJV)
> And David was greatly distressed; for the people spake of stoning him, because the soul of all the people was grieved, every man for his sons and for his daughters: but David encouraged himself in the LORD his God.
>
> Isaiah 41:10 (KJV)
> Fear thou not; for I am with thee: be not dismayed; for I am thy God: I will strengthen thee;

yea, I will help thee; yea, I will uphold thee with the right hand of my righteousness.

Hebrews 13:5-8 (NIV)
[5] Keep your lives free from the love of money and be content with what you have, because God has said, "Never will I leave you; never will I forsake you."
[6] So we say with confidence, "The Lord is my helper; I will not be afraid. What can mere mortals do to me?"
[7] Remember your leaders, who spoke the word of God to you. Consider the outcome of their way of life and imitate their faith.
[8] Jesus Christ is the same yesterday and today and forever.

I love the way someone beautifully explained Psalm 23:

[1] "The LORD is my shepherd";
~ *That's Relationship*!
"I shall not want."
~ *That's Supply!*
[2] "He maketh me to lie down in green pastures:"
~ *That's Rest!*
"He leadeth me beside the still waters."
~ *That's Refreshment!*
[3] "He restoreth my soul:"
~ *That's Healing!*
"He leadeth me in the paths of righteousness"
~ *That's Guidance!*
"for his name's sake."
~ *That's Purpose*

⁴ "Yea, though I walk through the valley of the shadow of death,"
   ~ *That's Testing!*
"I will fear no evil:"
   ~ *That's Protection!*
"for thou art with me;"
   ~ *That's Faithfulness!*
"thy rod and thy staff they comfort me."
   ~ *That's Discipline!*
⁵ "Thou preparest a table before me in the presence of mine enemies:"
   ~ *That's Favor!*
"thou anointest my head with oil;"
   ~ *That's Consecration!*
"my cup runneth over."
   ~ *That's Abundance!*
⁶ "Surely goodness and mercy shall follow me all the days of my life:"
   ~ *That's Blessings!*
"and I will dwell in the house of the LORD"
   ~ *That's Security!*
"forever."
   ~ *That's Eternity!*

(Author Unknown)

70. WHAT DO I NEED TO DO TO GO TO HEAVEN?

Your acceptance, faith and obedience in Jesus Christ are foundational steps to this destination. Faith produces works that glorify God and works demonstrates faith in Him. Heaven is a prepared place for a prepared people. We must make our decision here on earth and live according to God's instructions to secure this eternal reward.

There are no good works or deeds that can secure this destination. If good works could secure a place in heaven, than how much good works are good enough? Would feeding 100 or 100,000 hungry people, giving $20 or $200,000 to charity, or maybe going to church 30 or 300,000 times be enough; and where or when did God say this? We can only be sure of heaven's destination through God's instructions.

The Bible tells us that we must be godly sorrowful for the sins committed against God's holiness (this is repentance). Then, leaving sinful ways behind (sanctifying our lifestyle) to live according to God's plan. Lastly, have faith that Jesus' sacrifice of death on the cross pays our sin debt.

In conclusion, tombstones have two dates and a dash. The first date is our birthdate and the second is our departure (death) date. The most important of these three is the dash; which represents our entire life. Everyone will be accountable to God on their departure date for their dash (life) according to the B-I-B-L-E (**B**est / **I**nstructions / **B**efore / **L**eaving / **E**arth).

> Isaiah 55:6-7 (KJV)
> [6] Seek ye the LORD while he may be found, call ye upon him while he is near:
> [7] Let the wicked forsake his way, and the unrighteous man his thoughts: and let him return unto the LORD, and he will have mercy upon him; and to our God, for he will abundantly pardon.

Matthew 7:13-14 (NIV)
¹³ "Enter through the narrow gate. For wide is the gate and broad is the road that leads to destruction, and many enter through it.
¹⁴ But small is the gate and narrow the road that leads to life, and only a few find it.

John 3:16 (KJV)
For God so loved the world, that he gave his only begotten Son, that whosoever believeth in him should not perish, but have everlasting life.

John 14:6 (KJV)
Jesus saith unto him, I am the way, the truth, and the life: no man cometh unto the Father, but by me.

Acts 3:19 (KJV)
Repent ye therefore, and be converted, that your sins may be blotted out, when the Time of refreshing shall come from the presence of the Lord;

2 Corinthians 7:10 (NLT)
For the kind of sorrow God wants us to experience leads us away from sin and results in salvation. There's no regret for that kind of sorrow. But worldly sorrow, which lacks repentance, results in spiritual death.

1 Thessalonians 5:23 (KJV)
And the very God of peace sanctify you wholly; and I pray God your whole spirit and soul and body be preserved blameless unto the coming of our Lord Jesus Christ.

Hebrews 9:27-28 (KJV)
²⁷ And as it is appointed unto men once to die, but after this the judgment:
²⁸ So Christ was once offered to bear the sins of many; and unto them that look for him shall he appear the second time without sin unto salvation.

James 2:14-17 (KJV)
¹⁴ What doth it profit, my brethren, though a man say he hath faith, and have not works? can faith save him?
¹⁵ If a brother or sister be naked, and destitute of daily food,
¹⁶ And one of you say unto them, Depart in peace, be ye warmed and filled; notwithstanding ye give them not those things which are needful to the body; what doth it profit?
¹⁷ Even so faith, if it hath not works, is dead, being alone.

71. WHAT DOES IT MEAN TO BE A BELIEVER AND HOW DO I START A NEW LIFE IN CHRIST?

An <u>authentic Believer</u> (supporter, advocate, follower, or a disciple) is someone who has faith in and love Jesus Christ. Not only believe or have faith in Him, but is committed to trusting and obeying His commandments.

The Bible explains, *"No human can come to Jesus, except God draws them"*. Now it is your choice to make this decision to say: *"YES"* to God's invitation to salvation. You must repent (ask for forgiveness, have regret, and be sorry) to God. Ask Him to forgive you of all the sins you committed against Him, yourselves, and others. In doing this, you are telling God you have accepted His gift of eternal life through His Son Jesus Christ. Now by faith, you can live the abundant life He has planned for you!

Everyone desires to belong to a healthy family union that is based on true love. According to the gospel of St. John 3:3-5,16-17, Jesus stated to Nicodemus, *"Except a man be born again, he cannot see the kingdom of God. Except a man be born of water and of the Spirit, he cannot enter into the kingdom of God."* He further stated that *"God so loved the world, that he gave his only begotten Son, that whosoever believeth in him should not perish, but have everlasting life. For God sent not his Son into the world to condemn the world, but that the world through him might be saved."* God inspired the Apostle John to transcribe the conversation between Jesus and Nicodemus. This dialogue revealed the true love of God, the gift of God, how to obtain the gift, and the reward of receiving the gift. Examine the words of Christ to receive these promises. Then, believe this new birth in your heart for this wonderful born again experience!

John 1:12 (AMP)
But to as many as did receive and welcome Him, He gave the authority (power, privilege, right) to become the children of God, that is, to those who believe in (adhere to, trust in, and rely on) His name—

John 3:6-7 (KJV)
[6] That which is born of the flesh is flesh; and that which is born of the Spirit is spirit.

⁷ Marvel not that I said unto thee, Ye must be born again.

John 6:44 (KJV)
No man can come to me, except the Father which hath sent me draw him: and I will raise him up at the last day.

Romans 10:14-17 (KJV)
¹⁴ How then shall they call on him in whom they have not believed? and how shall they believe in him of whom they have not heard? and how shall they hear without a preacher?
¹⁵ And how shall they preach, except they be sent? as it is written, How beautiful are the feet of them that preach the gospel of peace, and bring glad tidings of good things!
¹⁶ But they have not all obeyed the gospel. For Esaias saith, Lord, who hath believed our report?
¹⁷ So then faith cometh by hearing, and hearing by the word of God.

2 Corinthians 5:17 (ASV)
Wherefore if any man is in Christ, he is a new creature: the old things are passed away; behold, they are become new.

Ephesians 2:8-9 (KJV)
⁸ For by grace are ye saved through faith; and that not of yourselves: it is the gift of God:
⁹ Not of works, lest any man should boast.

1 John 5:13 (KJV)
These things have I written unto you that believe on the name of the Son of God; that ye may know

that ye have eternal life, and that ye may believe on the name of the Son of God.

Revelation 22:17 (KJV)
And the Spirit and the bride say, Come. And let him that heareth say, Come. And let him that is athirst come. And whosoever will, let him take the water of life freely.

72. WHAT DOES IT MEAN TO BE SAVED?

To be saved means an individual who accepts Jesus as their Lord and Savior is saved (protected) from God's eternal wrath, punishment and judgment. Repentance mixed with faith in Jesus Christ saves us from these consequences. Un-repented sin will eternally separate individuals from God's love and mercy.

For clarity sake, you will hear individuals say "*We are saved from our sins.*" This statement isn't accurate. We are not saved from our sins; we are forgiven of sins.

As human beings we do not have to continue in sin; however this is always our challenge. Thankfully, God has made a way through repentance that we can get back on the right path by asking Him for forgiveness and help, if we fall into sin again. Please know, His death, burial, and resurrection completed what we need for salvation.

Proverbs 24:16 (NLT)
The godly may trip seven times, but they will get up again. But one disaster is enough to overthrow the wicked.

Romans 5:9 (KJV)
Much more then, being now justified by his blood, we shall be saved from wrath through him.

Romans 6:15-19 (TLB)
15 Does this mean that now we can go ahead and sin and not worry about it? (For our salvation does not depend on keeping the law but on receiving God's grace!) Of course not!
16 Don't you realize that you can choose your own master? You can choose sin (with death) or else obedience (with acquittal). The one to whom you offer yourself—he will take you and be your master, and you will be his slave.
17 Thank God that though you once chose to be slaves of sin, now you have obeyed with all your heart the teaching to which God has committed you.
18 And now you are free from your old master, sin; and you have become slaves to your new master, righteousness.
19 I speak this way, using the illustration of slaves and masters, because it is easy to understand: just as you used to be slaves to all kinds of sin, so now you must let yourselves be slaves to all that is right and holy.

1 Thessalonians 1:10 (TLB)
And they speak of how you are looking forward to the return of God's Son from heaven—Jesus, whom God brought back to life—and he is our only Savior from God's terrible anger against sin.

1 Timothy 2:3-4 (KJV)
3 For this is good and acceptable in the sight of God our Saviour;

⁴ Who will have all men to be saved, and to come unto the knowledge of the truth.

1 John 1:9 (KJV)
If we confess our sins, he is faithful and just to forgive us our sins, and to cleanse us from all unrighteousness.

73. WHAT ARE THE STEPS TO SALVATION?

Accepting Jesus saves us into a life of salvation (rescue from eternal punishment of sin) and He made it as simple, but profound, as steps to A-B-C:

Admit to God that you are a sinner.
Believe that Jesus died on the cross for your sins.
Confess your sins to Him for salvation.

Admit:

Psalm 41:4 (KJV)
I said, LORD, be merciful unto me: heal my soul; for I have sinned against thee.

Luke 18:13 (NIV)
"But the tax collector stood at a distance. He would not even look up to heaven, but beat his breast and said, 'God, have mercy on me, a sinner.'

Believe:

John 3:36 (KJV)
He that believeth on the Son hath everlasting life: and he that believeth not the Son shall not see life; but the wrath of God abideth on him.

Mark 9:24 (NIV)
Immediately the boy's father exclaimed, "I do believe; help me overcome my unbelief!"

Acts 10:43 (KJV)
To him give all the prophets witness, that through his name whosoever believeth in him shall receive remission of sins.

Confess:

Romans 10:9-10 (NLT)
[9] If you confess with your mouth that Jesus is Lord and believe in your heart that God raised him from the dead, you will be saved.
[10] For it is by believing in your heart that you are made right with God, and it is by confessing with your mouth that you are saved.

Acts 3:19 (KJV)
Repent ye therefore, and be converted, that your sins may be blotted out, when the Time of refreshing shall come from the presence of the Lord;

2 Corinthians 7:10 (NLT)
For the kind of sorrow God wants us to experience leads us away from sin and results in salvation. There's no regret for that kind of

sorrow. But worldly sorrow, which lacks repentance, results in spiritual death.

1 John 1:9 (KJV)
If we confess our sins, he is faithful and just to forgive us our sins, and to cleanse us from all unrighteousness.

74. DO I NEED THE HOLY SPIRIT?

Yes, every Believer needs the gift of the Holy Spirit (Holy Ghost). He is our Helper, Guide, Teacher, Intercessor, and Comforter. He empowers us to live holy and fight the good fight of faith!

We need the Holy Spirit because we need His power and strength. We have a real enemy, the devil; who speaks lies continuously. He say things like, "*Are you really saved*", "*Just try it one more time*", "*This will make you happy*" and "*No one cares about you anyway*." We need the Holy Spirit to give us power to resist the devil's lies and to stay on God's path.

Believers are also granted gifts of the Spirit according to 1 Corinthians 12:7-11. Then, the Holy Spirit produces: *love, joy, peace, patience, kindness, goodness, faithfulness, gentleness, and self-control*, according to Galatians 5:22-23.

John 16:7-13 (KJV)
Jesus said: [7] Nevertheless I tell you the truth; It is expedient for you that I go away: for if I go not away, the Comforter will not come unto you; but if I depart, I will send him unto you.

⁸ And when he is come, he will reprove the world of sin, and of righteousness, and of judgment:
⁹ Of sin, because they believe not on me;
¹⁰ Of righteousness, because I go to my Father, and ye see me no more;
¹¹ Of judgment, because the prince of this world is judged.
¹² I have yet many things to say unto you, but ye cannot bear them now.
¹³ Howbeit when he, the Spirit of truth, is come, he will guide you into all truth: for he shall not speak of himself; but whatsoever he shall hear, that shall he speak: and he will shew you things to come.

Acts 1:8 (KJV)
But ye shall receive power, after that the Holy Ghost is come upon you: and ye shall be witnesses unto me both in Jerusalem, and in all Judaea, and in Samaria, and unto the uttermost part of the earth.

Acts 2:38 (KJV)
Then Peter said unto them, Repent, and be baptized every one of you in the name of Jesus Christ for the remission of sins, and ye shall receive the gift of the Holy Ghost.

Romans 8:26 (KJV)
Likewise the Spirit also helpeth our infirmities: for we know not what we should pray for as we ought: but the Spirit itself maketh intercession for us with groanings which cannot be uttered.

1 Corinthians 12:8-11 (KJV)
[8] For to one is given by the Spirit the word of wisdom; to another the word of knowledge by the same Spirit;
[9] To another faith by the same Spirit; to another the gifts of healing by the same Spirit;
[10] To another the working of miracles; to another prophecy; to another discerning of spirits; to another divers kinds of tongues; to another the interpretation of tongues:
[11] But all these worketh that one and the selfsame Spirit, dividing to every man severally as he will.

Questions to the Author

I am a firm believer that someone else's experiences are helpful, because they can encourage, inspire, and build faith. My life is an open book and *I am not ashamed of the gospel of Jesus Christ, because it is the power of God unto salvation, to everyone that believeth.*

---

75. How did you get enough nerve to tell your story so freely?

No one saved me from my sins, but Jesus Christ alone. I am not ashamed of my past, because it brings God glory. My life is no longer my own. My boldness is for an individual who wants His redemption as well. I also learned not to be a people pleaser, but a God pleaser.

My parents loved me enough to tell me the truth. They did not and cannot stand before God to endure my sins. Christ paid a high price for my salvation which encourages me not to be ashamed to tell anyone of His marvelous works!

Romans 1:16 (KJV)
For I am not ashamed of this Good News about Christ. It is the power of God at work, saving everyone who believes—the Jew first and also the Gentile.

Romans 8:38-39 (TLB)
³⁸ For I am convinced that nothing can ever separate us from his love. Death can't, and life can't. The angels won't, and all the powers of hell itself cannot keep God's love away. Our fears for today, our worries about tomorrow,
³⁹ or where we are—high above the sky, or in the deepest ocean—nothing will ever be able to separate us from the love of God demonstrated by our Lord Jesus Christ when he died for us.

Matthew 10:32-33 (KJV)
³² Whosoever therefore shall confess me before men, him will I confess also before my Father which is in heaven.
³³ But whosoever shall deny me before men, him will I also deny before my Father which is in heaven.

Luke 9:26 (KJV)
For whosoever shall be ashamed of me and of my words, of him shall the Son of man be ashamed, when he shall come in his own glory, and in his Father's, and of the holy angels.

Ephesians 2:8-10 (KJV)
⁸ For by grace are ye saved through faith; and that not of yourselves: it is the gift of God:
⁹ Not of works, lest any man should boast.
¹⁰ For we are his workmanship, created in Christ Jesus unto good works, which God hath before ordained that we should walk in them.

2 Timothy 4:1-5 (NIV)
¹ In the presence of God and of Christ Jesus, who will judge the living and the dead, and in view of

his appearing and his kingdom, I give you this charge:
² Preach the word; be prepared in season and out of season; correct, rebuke and encourage—with great patience and careful instruction.
³ For the time will come when people will not put up with sound doctrine. Instead, to suit their own desires, they will gather around them a great number of teachers to say what their itching ears want to hear.
⁴ They will turn their ears away from the truth and turn aside to myths.
⁵ But you, keep your head in all situations, endure hardship, do the work of an evangelist, discharge all the duties of your ministry.

76. HOW DID YOU RECEIVE YOUR TOTAL HEALING AND STRENGTH TO REMAIN FREE FROM GOING BACK INTO A LESBIAN LIFESTYLE?

My healing, deliverance and wholeness from this lifestyle comes with much prayer, fasting and accountability. Keeping accountable to strong older Christian women was important for me, especially during my widowhood. They told me the truth no matter what. There were other sisters in Christ that mentored me as well. Having just one person wasn't fair if my problems became overwhelming for an individual. Besides, having more accountability kept me from starting any codependent relationships.

I had to sever ties with some family and old friends that were not healthy for my new life in Christ. For an example, at Jimmie's funeral, my schoolmate that I had my first female romantic affairs was in attendance. We talked and spent time together on several occasions thereafter; but I had to sever our friendship. During that time, I was still new in my relationship with Christ and too vulnerable. I am a firm believer that a person will either influence you their way or you will influence them your way. I did not want to give any room for satan to entice me. According to 2 Timothy 2:22, the bible warns us to: *"flee youthful lust"*; then Philippians 3:1-3 reminds us to *"put no confidence in the flesh."*

After God revealed my purpose in life, I sincerely began to study the Bible more passionately. I served in ministry before I was ordained; so this also helped me stay strong and busy for God.

Yes, there were a few bumps in the road like sexual temptations from recurring past lovers, seductive lesbian dreams, incubus violation experiences, loneness, and even depression; just to name a few. But, I am determined to make heaven my home and I know that *"I can do all things through Christ who strengthens me."* And, I know *"Freedom is a choice!"*

Jesus said:
Matthew 17:21 also Mark 9:29 (KJV)
And he said unto them, This kind can come forth by nothing, but by prayer and fasting.

Matthew 22:37-38 (KJV)
[37] Jesus said unto him, Thou shalt love the Lord thy God with all thy heart, and with all thy soul, and with all thy mind.
[38] This is the first and great commandment.

Philippians 4:13 (KJV)
I can do all things through Christ which strengtheneth me.

James 5:16 (KJV)
Confess your faults one to another, and pray one for another, that ye may be healed. The effectual fervent prayer of a righteous man availeth much.

1 John 4:4 (KJV)
Ye are of God, little children, and have overcome them: because greater is he that is in you, than he that is in the world.

Revelation 12:11 (ASV)
And they overcame him because of the blood of the Lamb, and because of the word of their testimony; and they loved not their life even unto death.

77. WHEN YOU WERE LIVING AS A LESBIAN, HOW DID YOUR FAMILY AND FRIENDS TREAT YOU?

For the most part my family and friends treated me with love and respect. They loved me for who I was, but took a firm stand against the lifestyle I chose. Living as a homosexual was not who I was created to be and homosexuality was not my identity. It was the behavior I chose to live. My parents continued to share bible passages with me to demonstrate the Love of God (but in my rebellious sin, I didn't think so).

Even though my parents did not agree with my choice of lifestyle, they did not reject nor stopped loving me as their child. My mom later flew to California to spend time with me and my female partner. We shopped, fellowshipped and had a wonderful time; but she never compromised her beliefs.

This was a great witness of her love not only for me, but also demonstrated her love for the soul of someone else's child. My parents allowed me to make my own choices, to do life God's way or my way. After all, it is my life and God gave me free will to choose.

> Joshua 24:15 (KJV)
> And if it seem evil unto you to serve the LORD, choose you this day whom ye will serve; whether the gods which your fathers served that *were* on the other side of the flood, or the gods of the Amorites, in whose land ye dwell: but as for me and my house, we will serve the LORD.

> Jeremiah 31:3(b) (KJV)
> : therefore with lovingkindness have I drawn thee.

78. WHAT INSPIRED YOU TO WRITE THIS BOOK?

This is a fulfilled prophecy of several prophets and prophetess (men and women according to ROMANS 12:6; *who receives divine information and revelation from God*). This is one of His assignments for me, to write books. So, I am being obedient to the messages I received. I was also instructed by a prophetess over 10 years ago to start journaling my life experiences. Now it has manifested, for such a time as this.

Through this assignment, God has ordained me to spread the gospel of Jesus Christ in so many unique circumstances to win souls. He has blessed me to have many wonderful opportunities to share my testimony to individuals and large audiences alike. This is so others can receive relational healing and wholeness as well.

Also, remembering my struggles to break free from the sins that had me bound in adultery, fornicating, homosexuality, lying and the list could go on; fuels my desire to reach individuals that are/were like me. I also read a book with testimonials of deliverance which tremendously helped me in my Christian journey to break free. Therefore, I feel an urgency to help someone else. If others did not share their experiences and ways of breaking free, then I wouldn't have known that this freedom could be for me.

Now my two favorite scriptures are: John 8:36 and Revelations 12:11.

Proverbs 11:30 (KJV)
The fruit of the righteous *is* a tree of life; and he that winneth souls *is* wise.

Isaiah 1:19-20 (KJV)
[19] If ye be willing and obedient, ye shall eat the good of the land:
[20] But if ye refuse and rebel, ye shall be devoured with the sword: for the mouth of the LORD hath spoken *it*.

Questions to the Author

Habakkuk 2:2 (AMP)
And the Lord answered me and said, Write the vision and engrave it so plainly upon tablets that everyone who passes may [be able to] read [it easily and quickly] as he hastens by.

John 8:36 (AMP)
So if the Son liberates you [makes you free men], then you are really and unquestionably free.

Luke 22:32 (KJV)
Jesus said: But I have prayed for thee, that thy faith fail not: and when thou art converted, strengthen thy brethren.

2 Corinthians 1:3-4 (NLT)
³ All praise to God, the Father of our Lord Jesus Christ. God is our merciful Father and the source of all comfort.
⁴ He comforts us in all our troubles so that we can comfort others. When they are troubled, we will be able to give them the same comfort God has given us.

Ephesians 5:10-11 (TLB)
¹⁰ Learn as you go along what pleases the Lord.
¹¹ Take no part in the worthless pleasures of evil and darkness, but instead, rebuke and expose them.

Revelation 1:3 (TLB)
If you read this prophecy aloud to the church, you will receive a special blessing from the Lord. Those who listen to it being read and do what it says will also be blessed. For the time is near when these things will all come true.

Revelation 12:11 (ASV)
And they overcame him because of the blood of the Lamb, and because of the word of their testimony; and they loved not their life even unto death.

As I Close:

I end this book with 78 questions:
7 = Completion and 8 = New Beginnings.

May you complete your healing in this season and embrace your New Beginnings in Jesus Name!

My Prayer for You:

'May you have an ear to hear God,
A heart to receive His instructions and
The will & strength to obey Him.

Godspeed...

Explanatory Notes:

Believers: Christian individuals that believe Jesus is the Son of God (John 3:16).

The Blood of Jesus: Jesus' shed blood on Calvary's cross for payment of our sins (Romans 5:7, 1 John 1:7 and Revelation 12:11).

God or God the Father: The almighty heavenly creator who created everything (Deuteronomy 4:35 & 39, John 1:3, Isaiah 46:9, Jeremiah 10:6-7, Malachi 2:10, Romans 11:33-36, 1 Corinthians 8:4, 6, Colossians 1:16 1 Timothy 2:5).

God, He, Him, Jesus, the Son of God and the Holy Spirit: are intentionally capitalized because of their deity.

God's Word: Is the Holy Bible (John 1:1, 2 Timothy 3:16 and 2 Peter 1:21-21).

Holy Spirit or Holy Ghost: Is also known as Comforter, Convicter of sin, Helper, Intercessor, Teacher, and Witness (just to name a few) - John 14:16 & 26, 15:26 & 16:7-11 16:13, Luke 1:35 & 3:22, Romans 8:16 & 26, 1 Corinthians 2:13, 2 Corinthians 13:14, and Hebrews 2:4 & 10:15.

Jesus: Is the Son of God who paid our sin debt and through His strips we are healed (Isaiah 9:6, Matthew 3:17 & 7:15, Mark 1:11, Luke 1:35 & 3:22, John 1:1-3 & 10, John 3:16,10:30, 13:13-14, 17:21 & 18:37, Philippians 2:5-8, 1 Timothy 2:5 & 6:15, Hebrews 1:2, Revelation 17:14 & 19:16). Jesus is also known as God in human flesh, The Word, King of kings and Lord of lords, Master, Mediator, Ruler, Savior, and Lamb of God.

The name satan: is intentionally not capitalized because he is not worth it.

Explanatory Notes

Trinity: Is God fashioned into three persons; God the Father, God the Son and God the Holy Spirit (Genesis 1:26, Matthew 28:19, and 1 Peter 1:2).

The will of God: His divine plan. For an example: this is similar to what we know as the last will and testament of an individual's desires for their property and possessions to go to their beneficiaries. God has given us His will through Old and New testaments, for evidence of His divine plan for each of us (Micah 6:8, Psalm 40:8, Psalm 138:8, Isaiah 55:11, Matthew 6:10, 1 Thessalonians 5:18, Romans 12:2, Ephesians 5:17, James 4:15 and 1 John 2:17).

To book Pastor Pamela R. Poston for speaking engagements, please send request to:

> Highways & Hedges Outreach Ministries
> PO Box 70222
> Las Vegas, NV 89170

If you have a testimony of relational healing or freedom from homosexuality that you would like to share, please write our ministry. Also, if you accepted Jesus as your Lord and Savior or rededicated your life to Him after reading this book, please let me know. Write me at:

Ministry@highways4JC.com

www.ingramcontent.com/pod-product-compliance
Lightning Source LLC
Chambersburg PA
CBHW061256110426
42742CB00012BA/1936